Schöningh

TEACHERS' BOOK

Discover ...

TOPICS FOR ADVANCED LEARNERS

edited by Engelbert Thaler

Australia and New Zealand

Neither Down nor Under

by Rainer H. Berthelmann

Sprachliche Betreuung: Simone Duxbury-Ziemer

www.schoeningh-schulbuch.de
Schöningh Verlag, Jühenplatz 1–3, 33098 Paderborn

Druck 5 4 3 2 / Jahr 2014 13 12 11
Die letzte Zahl bezeichnet das Jahr dieses Druckes.

Umschlaggestaltung: Franz-Josef Domke, Hannover
Umschlagabbildung: © Wildlife/M. Harvey (l.); © picture-alliance/Bildagentur Huber (r.)
Druck und Bindung: westermann Druck GmbH, Braunschweig

ISBN 978-3-14-040105-0

Inhaltsverzeichnis

Die didaktische Konzeption

Die Themenheftreihe *Discover* ... richtet sich an Schülerinnen und Schüler der Sekundarstufe II und bereitet in Anlehnung an die Einheitlichen Prüfungsanforderungen in der Abiturprüfung (EPA) und die Rahmenrichtlinien der einzelnen Bundesländer interkulturell relevante, Jugendliche interessierende Themen methodisch-didaktisch auf.

Der Einstieg in das Thema, das in mehrere Kapitel untergliedert ist, erfolgt über eine Doppelseite „Getting started" mit Bildmaterial und einigen Einstiegsaufgaben. Die Texte weisen unterschiedliche Längen auf, sind aber insgesamt nicht zu lang und berücksichtigen verschiedene Textsorten. Reichlich Bildmaterial (Fotos, Zeichnungen, Cartoons, Grafiken, Tabellen, Karten etc.) ist funktional in die Texte und Aufgabenapparate integriert.

Der Aufbau der einzelnen Texte ermöglicht einen klar strukturierten Unterricht mit drei Phasen: *pre, while* und *post reading*. *Pre-reading*-Aufgaben führen zum Text hin, rufen das Vorwissen ab und bauen Erwartungshaltungen auf. Der eigentliche Leseprozess wird im Sinne eines *guided reading* durch gelegentliche Lesebeobachtungsaufgaben und (sparsame) Annotationen in den Fußnoten unterstützt. Im abschließenden Aufgabenapparat unter dem Titel „Activities" werden alle Fragen zu thematisch zusammengehörigen Blöcken mit einer kurzen inhaltlichen Überschrift in der Randspalte zusammengefasst. Diese Aufgaben lassen sich den drei maßgeblichen Bereichen zuordnen:

a) Inhalt (*comprehension*)
b) Struktur, Intention, Stil, Sprache (*analysis*)
c) Evaluation, eigene Meinungsäußerung, sprachproduktive kreative Aufgaben (*evaluation and creation*).

Prof. Dr. Engelbert Thaler, Herausgeber

Aufbau des Schülerhefts

Das Schülerbuch „Australia and New Zealand – Neither Down nor Under" spricht Schüler der Klassenstufen 10 bis 13 mit speziell für sie ausgewählten Texten an. Im Vordergrund stehen jugendgemäße Themen wie die Nationale Jugendwoche in Australien, Sport, Film und der Lebensalltag in beiden Ländern. Aber auch die verschiedenen Möglichkeiten, die gelungene Durchmischung von britischer, multikultureller und „exotischer" Kultur (Aborigines bzw. Māori) in Australien und Neuseeland als Backpacker, Schüler, Student oder Tourist selbst zu erleben, nehmen einen breiten Raum ein. Den unerlässlichen geschichtlichen, politischen und sozialen Hintergrund bieten kurze Texte auch zu diesen Themen.

Das übergeordnete Hauptziel des Kurses besteht darin, die Schüler erfahren zu lassen, dass sowohl Australien als auch Neuseeland nicht zu den „kleineren" oder gar „unterentwickelten" Ländern gehören. Dieser Eindruck kann nur dann entstehen, wenn aufgrund der außerordentlich großen Entfernung der Länder Informationen über sie nur sporadisch in deutsche Medien gelangen. Im Gegenteil, diese Länder besitzen eine sehr interessante multikulturelle Gesellschaft, eine hoch entwickelte Wirtschaft und eine überaus reizvolle Natur. Ihre Menschen sind aufgeschlossen und offen für den Kontakt mit anderen Ländern.

Das Schülerbuch umfasst den regionalen Gegebenheiten entsprechend zwei Teile. Der Kurs „Australia" mit ausführlichen Beiträgen zur Geschichte und Gegenwart dieses einen ganzen Kontinent bildenden Staats nimmt etwa zwei Drittel ein, „Neuseeland" den Rest des Buchs. Der gegenüber vergleichbaren Kursheften relativ größere Anteil Neuseelands ist damit zu begründen, dass das kleine Land mit seinen nur etwas mehr als 4 Millionen Einwohnern eine nicht geringe politische und wirtschaftliche Rolle in der Welt spielt. Mehr noch, es steht in mancher Hinsicht sogar mit an der Spitze: Beispielsweise hat Neuseeland als erstes Land der Welt das Frauenwahlrecht eingeführt, die Regierung verfolgt seit langem eine erfolgreiche Minderheitenpolitik in Bezug auf die Māori und ihre Sprache, die Energiewirtschaft kommt ohne Nuklearenergie aus.

Beide Kurse sind in der gleichen Weise aufgebaut. Zwei Unterrichtsschritte bilden jeweils den Einstieg:
- das methodisch unterschiedlich gestaltete Erfassen der Vorkenntnisse der Kursgruppe und das damit einhergehende Abstecken der Lernziele, und
- die Hinführung zum Thema über Bilder, geografische und politische Karten sowie eine steckbriefartige Information über die Länder.

Dann folgen jeweils mehrseitige Kapitel zu ausgewählten Themen. Die Texte jedes Kapitels sind reich illustriert und werden mithilfe der in den *Activities* aufgeführten Aufgaben abgearbeitet. In den Aufgaben werden die drei Anforderungsbereiche sowie die Forderungen der Bildungsstandards für Englisch und des Gemeinsamen Europäischen Referenzrahmens für Sprachen angemessen berücksichtigt. Besonderes Augenmerk wird dabei auf die Nutzung einer breiten Palette von Medien gelegt. Viele Aufgaben verweisen auf Möglichkeiten der Themenerweiterung durch Internetrecherchen und geben Hinweise und Links dazu. Auf diese Weise können die Lerner in selbstständiger Arbeit einige Themen ihrer Wahl über das Schülerbuch hinaus ergründen und die jeweils geeignete Form der Präsentation ihrer Ergebnisse in der Klasse bestimmen.

Nahezu alle Seiten des Schülerbuchs sind darüber hinaus mit Illustrationen versehen, die die andersartige Kultur anschaulich darstellen, die Schüler zu weiteren Aktivitäten anregen oder auch „nur“ eine positive affektive Einstellung zum Land erzeugen sollen.

Aufbau des Lehrerhefts

Diese Lehrerhandreichung
- gibt methodische Hinweise zur Aufbereitung der Themen und zur Behandlung der im Schülerbuch enthaltenen Texte,
- erläutert die im Schülerbuch gestellten Aufgaben, legt Lösungen vor und unterbreitet Lösungsvorschläge,
- vermittelt über die im Schülerbuch enthaltenen Fakten und Daten hinaus für die Lehrkraft wichtige Hintergrundinformationen zu den behandelten Themen und zeigt Alternativen auf.

Diesen Ansprüchen wird das vorliegende Lehrerheft gerecht. Es folgt strikt dem Aufbau des Schülerkurses. Zu allen Kapiteln wird eine deutschsprachige Einleitung in das jeweilige Thema gegeben, die weitere Hintergrundinformationen für die Lehrkraft sowie eine Vielzahl von Webseiten und Literaturhinweisen enthält. Danach folgen zu jedem Text (Fremdtexte der verschiedenen Sorten, Autorentexte wie die Infobox oder der Textvorspann) spezielle Erläuterungen und methodische Hinweise zur Arbeit mit ihnen, die selbstverständlich nur als Anregung dienen und oft schon selbst Alternativen eröffnen.

Die in den *Activities* gestellten Aufgaben werden im Lehrerheft in der Regel detailliert beantwortet, mit Beispiellösungen versehen bzw. erläutert. Insofern die Lösung einer Aufgabe mit einem Arbeitsblatt verbunden wird, erfolgt ein Hinweis auf eines der 17 Worksheets.

Beide Kurse runden die Behandlung ihrer Themen mit einem Quiz ab, in dem das erworbene Wissen abgefragt wird. Allerdings können sich die Fragen des Quiz nur auf die im Kurs vermittelten Daten und Fakten beziehen. Das in selbstständiger Arbeit erworbene Additivum könnte Bestandteil einer Erweiterung oder eines von der Klasse selbst erstellten Fragebogens sein.

Tabellarische Textübersicht

Australia – My First Encounter

Autor, Text	Inhaltliche Schwerpunkte	Textsorte/ Medium	Wortzahl
I never knew this about Australia	Allgemeine geografische Angaben und Bevölkerung Australiens	Informative text	142
Kevin Rudd: Diverse and Breathtaking Landscapes and Nature	Stellungnahme des Premierministers zur Rolle von Landschaft und Natur in Australien	Argumentative text/Website	53

Young People in Australia

Autor, Text	Inhaltliche Schwerpunkte	Textsorte/ Medium	Wortzahl
National Youth Week	Ziele, Programm, Veranstalter, Teilnehmer und Sponsoren der NYW	Website	438
I never knew this about Australia	Informationen über die Auszeichnung „Young Australian of the Year"	Informative text	54
Kate Ellis	Einschätzung der Bedeutung, die die NYW für Australien hat, durch die Kultusministerin von NSW	Political statement	115
NYW 2008 in review	Rückblick auf die NYW 2008	Website	115
National Youth Week: Talent Comps – 2008 Winners	Vorstellung von vier Siegern der NYW 2008	Website	242

Living in Australia

Autor, Text	Inhaltliche Schwerpunkte	Textsorte/ Medium	Wortzahl
News around Australia	Sieben Artikel zu verschiedenen Alltagsthemen	Newspaper articles	
A land where all kids can play	Bericht eines libanesischen Einwanderers über seinen erfolgreichen Start in Australien	Newspaper article	147
Slaying the hackers	Bericht über Störungen der Abwasserpumpanlagen in Maroochydore durch Computerhacker	Newspaper article	173
The day the city came out to say thanks	Bericht über die Begrüßungsparade der Olympiateilnehmer von Peking 2008 in Sydney	Newspaper article	162
You don't have to live in Melbourne	Leserbrief mit einer Stellungnahme zur Entwicklung Melbournes als Megacity	Newspaper article	166
Ur kid's L8 4 skool	Bericht über die Nutzung moderner Medien in der Schule	Newspaper article	135
Postgraduate Education – All abroad	Erlebnisbericht einer kanadischen Studentin im Postgraduiertenkolleg	Newspaper article	123
Their goes you're grammar	Bericht über mangelnde Sprachkompetenz von Schulabgängern	Newspaper article	126
I never knew this about Australia	Hintergrundinformationen zu den in den sieben Artikeln behandelten Themen	Informative text	297

Australian Culture

Autor, Text	Inhaltliche Schwerpunkte	Textsorte/ Medium	Wortzahl
Aboriginal Art	Ausführungen über einen indigenen Künstler der Missionsschule in Ernabella	Newspaper article	247
Aboriginal Music	Selbstdarstellung der Band „Yothu Yindi"	Website	271
A. B. Paterson: Waltzing Matilda	Eine Einführung in das Lied und der Song als Lückentext	Song text	186
Brett Whiteley – One of Australia's Avant-Garde Artists	Beschreibung des künstlerischen Werdegangs und einiger Aktivitäten von Brett Whiteley	Biographical text	241
Melina Marchetta: Finnikin of the Rock	Anfang des Buchs „Finnikin of the Rock"	Novel	318
Baz Luhrmann: Australia	Besprechung des Films „Australia"	Website	272
"Neighbours" – An Australian TV Soap	Bericht über die Neighbours Night, eine Fanveranstaltung der TV-Serie	Website	228

Multicultural Australia

Autor, Text	Inhaltliche Schwerpunkte	Textsorte/ Medium	Wortzahl
Peter Jensen: What Place Multiculturalism?	Ein Erzbischof äußert sich zur multikulturellen Entwicklung in Australien	Essay	397
Quyang Yu: Far and Near	Kurzes Gedicht über die Befindlichkeit eines asiatischen Einwanderers in Australien	Poem	26
I never knew this about Australia	Informationen über die Einwanderergenerationen und die vorherrschenden Religionen in Australien	Informative text	196
Tim Winton: Neighbours	Der Text erzählt die Geschichte eines jungen Paars, das in ein Viertel von europäischen Immigranten einzieht	Short story	1237
E. Himmelreich: City Welcomes New Citizens	Bericht über die offizielle Begrüßung neuer australischer Bürger aus verschiedenen Herkunftsländern	Newspaper article	284
Australia and Me – Interview with Stephen O'Grady	Interview mit einem irischen Einwanderer	Interview	366
A. Radle: Letters from Immigrants (I)	Kurzer Lebensbericht einer Immigrantin aus Österreich	Letter	309
B. Schwaerzler: Letters from Immigrants (II)	Kurzer Lebensbericht eines Einwanderers aus Deutschland	Letter	274
Citizenship Testing	Zusammenfassung der Bestimmungen für den Einwanderungstest und kurze Übersicht über die offiziellen australischen Werte	Factual text	254

Outback but not Back of Bourke

Autor, Text	Inhaltliche Schwerpunkte	Textsorte/ Medium	Wortzahl
S. Kilgariff: School of the Air	Brief einer Schülerin über die hinter ihr liegende Zeit als Teilnehmerin an der School of the Air	Letter	396
I never knew this about Australia	Aus der Geschichte der School of the Air	Informative text	71

Autor, Text	Inhaltliche Schwerpunkte	Textsorte/ Medium	Wortzahl
School of the Air	Antworten auf Fragen nach der Art des Unterrichts, der Anzahl der unterrichteten Schüler u.a.m.	Informative text/ FAQs	293
Royal Flying Doctor Service	Informationen aus einem Faltblatt über die Geschichte und Gegenwart des RFDS	Factual text	685
The Outback – Pearl and Peril of Australia	Kurze Beschreibung einiger Gefahren im Outback	Factual text	182
I never knew this about Australia	Informationen über Vegetationszonen, Klima, Natur und Wirtschaft im Outback	Informative text	271

The Making of Australia

Autor, Text	Inhaltliche Schwerpunkte	Textsorte/ Medium	Wortzahl
The Rainbow Snake – Aboriginal Dreamtime Story	Nacherzählung einer der für die Mythologie der Aborigines bedeutendsten traditionellen Geschichten	Folk tale	295
I never knew this about Australia	Informationen über die Herkunft und Entwicklung der Völker der Aboriginals und Torres Strait Islanders	Informative text	420
A Nation is Born	Kurze Darstellung der Entdeckung Australiens durch Willem Janszoon und James Cook	Factual text	269
Jane Harrison: Stolen	Kurzer Ausschnitt aus dem Schauspiel: Szene zwischen einem Mädchen indigener Herkunft und ihren Adoptiveltern	Play	307
Burnum Burnum: The Burnum Burnum Declaration	In die Form einer scharfen politischen Satire gekleidete Deklaration der Annexion Großbritanniens durch die Aboriginal people	Political satire	328

Politics and Economy

Autor, Text	Inhaltliche Schwerpunkte	Textsorte/ Medium	Wortzahl
Kevin Rudd: The Nation Apologises	Regierungserklärung des Premierministers zur Entschuldigung bei den über mehr als 200 Jahre unterdrückten indigenen Völkern Australiens	Political speech	287
Oodgeroo Noonuccal: I Am Proud	Gedicht von Oodgeroo Noonuccal über den ungebrochenen Stolz der Ureinwohner Australiens	Poem	108
Australia's Government	Ausschnitt aus der Broschüre "Becoming an Australian Citizen" über die politische Verfassung des Landes	Factual text	308
Politics and Economy in the 20th Century	Kurzer Abriss der Wirtschafts- und Parteiengeschichte Australiens	Factual text	364
Australia – Neither Down nor Under	Einschätzung der wirtschaftlichen Stärke Australiens aus internationaler Sicht	Factual text	310

New Zealand – My First Encounter

Autor, Text	Inhaltliche Schwerpunkte	Textsorte/ Medium	Wortzahl
I never knew this about New Zealand	Informationen über Geografie, Besiedlung und Bevölkerung Neuseelands; Erläuterung der Polysemie des Worts „Kiwi“	Informative text	308
The Legend of Māui	Sehr kurze Wiedergabe der mythologischen Geschichte über die Entstehung der beiden Inseln	Fictional text	126
Haere Mai! – Te Reo Māori	Ausführungen über die Sprache und die Sprecher des Māori	Factual text	268
Treaty of Waitangi	Die englische Version des von William Hobson signierten Vertrags zur Übernahme Neuseelands durch die britische Krone	Law text/ Contract	374
Parihaka – A Symbol of Protest	Beschreibung des Widerstands neuseeländischer Stämme gegen den Vertrag von Waitangi	Newspaper article	331

Māori Then and Today

Autor, Text	Inhaltliche Schwerpunkte	Textsorte/ Medium	Wortzahl
I never knew this about New Zealand	Informationen über die Rolle der Māori im heutigen Neuseeland	Informative text	305
Did you know?	Abdruck des längsten Ortsnamens in Neuseeland	Place name	53
Māori Ethnic Population – Te Momo Iwi Māori	Statistische Angaben über die Entwicklung der Māori-Population zu Beginn des 21. Jahrhunderts	Statistical data	124
Māori Culture in New Zealand and Abroad	Fünf Artikel über die Rolle der Māori in der Gegenwart	Newspaper articles, etc.	
Feel the spirit – Manaakitanga	Erläuterung des Manaakitanga, der traditionellen Begrüßungszeremonie, und der Werte der Māori	Brochure	144
Leaders get experience	Bericht über Māori- und Pasifikastudenten, die an einem *leadership programme* in Auckland teilnehmen	Newspaper article	83
tamariki on TV	Bericht über jugendliche Teilnehmer an einer Māori-Kulturgruppe in London	Newspaper article	126
Kiwis one short in medal hunt – Paralympics	Bericht über die von einem Māorisportler unglücklich verpasste Medaille während der Paralympischen Spiele in Peking 2008	Newspaper article	162
Māori Heritage in Great Britain	Bericht über die Überführung eines wertvollen alten *pouhaki*, eines Totempfahls der Māori	Newspaper article	169

Schools in New Zealand

Autor, Text	Inhaltliche Schwerpunkte	Textsorte/ Medium	Wortzahl
A High School Year in Aotearoa	Anonymisierter Brief einer deutschen Schülerin, den sie während ihres Aufenthalts an einer neuseeländischen High School geschrieben hat	Letter	491
New Plymouth Girls' High School	Auszüge aus dem Jahrbuch mit Beschreibung der Ziele der Schule	Brochure	174
Rotorua Boys' High School	Auszug aus dem Brief des Schulleiters an die Eltern	Letter	79
Rotorua Boys' High School	Auszug aus dem Schuljahrbuch: Prinzipien und Werte	Brochure/School Year Book	241

Sports and Leisure Activities

Autor, Text	Inhaltliche Schwerpunkte	Textsorte/ Medium	Wortzahl
New Zealanders Are People of Action	Beschreibung der sportlichen Aktivitäten der Neuseeländer	Newspaper article	250
Bungee Jumping	Anonymisierte Blogeinträge von Jugendlichen über ihren ersten Bungeesprung	Blog posts	143

Films and Books

Autor, Text	Inhaltliche Schwerpunkte	Textsorte/ Medium	Wortzahl
I never knew this about New Zealand	Informationen über die bedeutendsten Filmproduktionen Neuseelands und die ihnen zugrunde liegenden Romane	Informative text	280
Films Important to New Zealand's Economy	Bericht über neuere neuseeländische Filmproduktionen	Magazine	220
Whale Rider	Mitschrift vom Beginn des Films „Whale Rider"	Film transcript	256

Politics and People

Autor, Text	Inhaltliche Schwerpunkte	Textsorte/ Medium	Wortzahl
How Government Works	Ausschnitt aus dem Text des von der Regierung herausgegebenen Faltblatts „New Zealand in Outline" über die politische Verfassung des Landes	Factual text	199
I never knew this about New Zealand	Informationen über die politischen Wahlen und den Anteil an Frauen in der Politik Neuseelands	Informative text	183
H. Clark: Quotation	Kurzes Zitat aus dem folgenden Interview, in dem Helen Clark die Rolle des Landes in der Welt beschwört	Interview	78
Central Government – Prime Ministers	Helen Clark beantwortet die Frage, welche drei Dinge auf ihrer Agenda für das Land an vorderster Stelle stehen	Interview	272

Women play an important role	Informationen über die Geschichte des Frauenrechts in Neuseeland und die Rolle der Frauen in Neuseeland heute	Informative text	275

Not Just Sheep and Wool

Autor, Text	Inhaltliche Schwerpunkte	Textsorte/ Medium	Wortzahl
Innovative Economy	Zwei Zeitungsartikel über moderne Technologien in Neuseeland	Newspaper articles	
Harvesting power from the skies	Bericht über die besondere Förderung der Erzeugung von Windenergie	Newspaper article	230
Electric cars set for Kiwi trials next year	Bericht über die Anstrengungen des Landes, emissionsfreie Automobile zu produzieren	Newspaper article	106
New Zealand's Import and Export	Zwei statistische Darstellungen und Illustrationen zum Thema Import und Export Neuseelands	Graphs/ Statistics	
I never knew this about New Zealand	Informationen über Agrarwirtschaft und Industrie Neuseelands	Informative text	147

New Zealand's Nature – Beauty and Beast

Autor, Text	Inhaltliche Schwerpunkte	Textsorte/ Medium	Wortzahl
New Zealand's Hazards	Beschreibung der verschiedenen natürlichen Gefahren in Neuseeland	Factual text	455
New Zealand's Beautiful Landscapes	Vier Artikel über einige der sehenswerten Landschaften	Articles/ Newspaper	
A land full of natural beauty	Der Text beschreibt die Mannigfaltigkeit der wunderbaren Landschaften Neuseelands	Brochure	201
Tongariro National Park	Die Broschüre des Nationalparks beschreibt u. a. Orte, die durch den Film „The Lord of the Rings" bekannt wurden	Brochure	187
Shrinking NZ glaciers are smallest since records began	Der Artikel geht auf das durch die globale Erwärmung herbeigeführte Abschmelzen der großen Gletscher Neuseelands ein	Newspaper article	133
Iron like Zion	Der Artikel in einer Outdoor-Zeitschrift beschreibt die herrliche Landschaft am Iron Gates Gorge	Magazine	254
The Top Ten Eco-Experiences in New Zealand	Aufzählung von zehn sehenswerten Landschaften in Neuseeland	Magazine	321

Australia – Getting started

Das *Commonwealth of Australia* ist ein industriell hoch entwickeltes Land und führend in der Welt in mehreren Sektoren der landwirtschaftlichen Branche. Trotzdem ist es vor allem wohl aufgrund seiner großen Entfernung von Europa in den Medien und bei vielen Menschen nicht so präsent wie andere Industriestaaten.
Nichtsdestoweniger ist Australien für viele ein „Geheimtipp". Da gibt es exotische Landschaften, viele Naturdenkmäler, allen voran der erst von den Briten sogenannte Ayers Rock (heute Uluru), übersprudelnd lebendige Städte, insbesondere die Millionenstädte Sydney und Melbourne mit ihren Sehenswürdigkeiten. Aber es ist auch ein Land mit geringer Arbeitslosigkeit und darum großen Chancen, einen Job zu bekommen. Auch Schüler und Studenten verbringen gern ein halbes oder ganzes Jahr an Australiens Hochschulen und High Schools.
Über Australien, seine Menschen, Geschichte und Natur gibt es unzählige Nachschlagemöglichkeiten im Internet und diverse Bücher in jeder Bibliothek. Eine empfehlenswerte Quelle mit zuverlässigen Angaben über viele Aspekte des australischen Lebens ist die Webpräsenz der Charles Sturt University, die zehn Standorte in Australien hat und eine der größten des Landes ist: http://www.csu.edu.au/australia/. Darüber hinaus werden in diesem Material für die Hand des Lehrers immer wieder Hinweise auf Literatur und Internetseiten gegeben.
Zum ersten Mal auf der Seite 8 des Schülerbuchs taucht eines der unregelmäßig verteilten grünen „Eselsohren" auf. Sie sind *eye catcher*, die Tipps, Worterklärungen und andere nützliche Hinweise vermitteln, die die Leser des Hefts, auch ohne sie gründlicher zu lesen, unterschwellig wahrnehmen und so ihr landeskundliches Wissen erweitern können.
Möglichst noch vor der Beschäftigung mit dem Kursthema „Australien" sollte sich die Lehrkraft (am besten im Vorjahr) eine grobe Orientierung verschaffen, welches allgemeine Vorwissen die Kursgruppe darüber besitzt und wie motiviert sie ist, sich mit *Down Under* zu beschäftigen. Als motivierender Einstieg in das Thema zu Beginn des Kurses können die Fotos und Aufgaben auf den Seiten 6 und 7 dienen.

Solution

Activity p. 7

The pictures on this double page show scenes which are typical of Australia. Describe or guess what the people are doing. Which of the pictures arouses your particular interest? Why? Discuss.

The students will, of course, give individual speculative answers to describe what the people in the pictures are doing. They should, however, understand why the scenes are typical of Australia.
Pages 6 and 7 show one big picture of the City of Sydney. This picture was taken at a point next to the famous Opera House. In the background, you see Circular Quay, Sydney's heavily-frequented central ferry station, and behind it, the CBD (Central Business District). The people in the foreground of the big photo are just relaxing near the harbour or perhaps are waiting for the beginning of a performance in the Opera House.
Furthermore, there are three photos representing typical scenes in Australia: 1) an indigenous man playing the didgeridoo for a tip, which is readily given by tourists (this represents the darker side of Aboriginal life); 2) young Asian Australians celebrating a traditional holiday (this represents the large proportion of immigrants in Australia's population); 3) two young Germans who visited Down Under as backpackers (this represents the international, and also German, interest in the country).

Australia – My First Encounter

Jugendgemäße Themen setzen den Einstieg fort: Autokennzeichen, eine lustige Karte sowie die atemberaubenden Landschaften und Tiere von Australien.

Number Plates of Australian Vehicles

Die Schüler sollen die *number plates* den einzelnen Staaten zuordnen. Außer den *Activities* und den Nummernschildern der sechs Staaten und zwei Territorien, die das *Commonwealth of Australia* bilden, finden die Schüler auf der Seite 8 das Foto eines „*Drive on Left*"-Hinweisschildes, denn in Australien gilt wie im Mutterland Großbritannien Linksverkehr.
Die Bilder bieten weitere Sprechanlässe, z. B. darüber, wo überall in der Welt Linksverkehr herrscht (u. a. Indien, Südafrika, Zypern, aber nicht in den USA).

Solutions

Activities p. 8

1. **Which stereotypes do you connect with 'Oz'? Do you think that, after you have looked at Australia more closely, your stereotypes will dissolve? Give reasons.**
   First of all, the teacher should make sure that everybody understands the strine (= Australian slang) word "Oz".
   Students, like most other people, usually associate Australia with stereotypes such as Ayers Rock/Uluru, aboriginal culture, kangaroos, Sydney Harbour Bridge, etc. These "stereotypes" are typical features of Australia, so in effect one cannot even speak of "clichés". However, they are not the only famous characteristics or sights the country (and continent) has to offer. For this reason, the "stereotypes" will probably not dissolve but be seen as some of the typical features of the country.
2. **The eight number plates stand for Australia's states and territories. Find out their names with the help of the map on the next page.**
   XTH 241 – South Australia (nickname: The Festival State)
   286 GKW – Queensland (nickname: Sunshine State)
   WHK 950 – Victoria (nickname: The Place To Be)
   YPD 640 – Australian Capital Territory (nickname: The Nation's Capital)
   903-992 – Northern Territory (nickname: Outback Australia)
   AQ 41 UB – New South Wales (nicknames: First or Premier State; here not mentioned on the plate)
   FR 7949 – Tasmania (nickname: Your Natural State)
   1CMN 505 – Western Australia (nickname: Golden State; here not mentioned on the plate)
3. **Before you read the yellow box below, have a guess:**
   What is the area of Australia?
   7,686,850 km^2
   How far away is the continent from Europe?
   About 16,000 km
   What is Australia's population?
   22 million people (November 2009)
   What does the continent's name mean?
   The word "Australia" is derived from a Latin word meaning "south".

Some of the students will probably know these answers more or less correctly. The main task of these questions, therefore, is to concentrate the students' reading attention on the issues given.

I never knew this about Australia

Im gesamten Schülerbuch werden in den gelben Kästchen „I never knew this about Australia" (bzw. im zweiten Teil „I never knew this about New Zealand") Informationen über das Land gegeben, die zusätzliches Hintergrundwissen vermitteln oder Ergänzungen zu den Lesetexten darstellen. Sie werden nur zum Teil direkt abgefragt. Es wird jedoch erwartet, dass die Schüler sie stets lesen (in der Regel als Still- oder Hausarbeit) und in ihre Antworten einbeziehen, wenn sie die Aufgaben der *Activities* bearbeiten. Die Abbildung in den gelben Infokästchen zeigt das Nationalemblem Australiens.

Maps of Australia

Auf der Seite 9 sind zwei Karten kontrastiv gegenübergestellt. „McArthur's Universal Corrective Map of the World" stellt die Welt sozusagen auf den Kopf. Stuart McArthur hat sie 1973 angefertigt, als er als 15-jähriger Austauschschüler in Japan der Hänseleien seiner Mitschüler überdrüssig war, er käme doch *„from the bottom of the world"* (dt. vergleichbar mit dem Ausdruck „vom A... der Welt"). Diese Sichtweise spiegelt sich auch in dem in Europa geläufigen Ausdruck *Down Under* wider. Er wurde früher tatsächlich mit einer pejorativen Nuance gebraucht. Im australischen Englisch ist dieser Begriff ursprünglich nicht bekannt gewesen und wurde erst mit zunehmendem nationalen Selbstbewusstsein zur Abgrenzung vom „Rest der Welt" benutzt. Verschiedene Varianten der oben erwähnten Karte sind als touristische Mitbringsel sehr beliebt.
Als Hintergrundwissen für die Lehrkraft oder als zusätzlicher Lesetext kann der folgende Kommentar zu McArthurs Karte gelesen werden:

> "A number of years ago I was conducting a seminar for government managers at a conference site in West Virginia. We shared the facility with a small international conference, whose participants had met the year before in Geneva, the year before that in Paris. Here they were in the lovely hills of West Virginia but already they were promoting their next year's meeting in Alice Springs, Australia. The Australian contingent had posted a map on the door of their main meeting room – McArthur's Universal Corrective Map of the World. It attempted to correct the old Mercator projection of the world that was so familiar to all of us. It showed the South on top, with Australia in the center of the map. The map read, in part, "South is superior. South dominates! Long live AUSTRALIA – RULER OF THE UNIVERSE!!" Our group of managers chuckled over that, but also engaged in a spirited discussion of perceptions, world views, and the importance of – at least occasionally – seeing things differently. I left the seminar with the humbling knowledge that the discussion about McArthur's map was the best learning of the week."
>
> Ron Rago, GTN (The Government Training News is a monthly newsletter that features stories about public sector learning and organisational development.)
> from: http://odtmaps.com/what_they_are_saying/mcarthur-reader-comments.asp

Die zweite Abbildung ist eine politische Karte des Kernlands von Australien. Die vielen zum *Commonwealth* gehörenden Inseln sind, außer Tasmanien, nicht berücksichtigt. Die Schüler können ihr die Namen der acht politischen Verwaltungseinheiten des Landes (Staaten bzw. Territorien) und deren Hauptstädte entnehmen.

Diverse and Breathtaking Landscapes and Nature

Die sechs Landschaftsfotografien auf Seite 10 repräsentieren die wesentlichen Vegetationszonen Australiens:

- die *Blue Mountains* stehen für die Baumzone im australischen Busch entlang der Ostküsten des Landes,
- die grasenden Schafe sind charakteristisch für die landwirtschaftliche Nutzung ausgedehnter Gebiete im küstennahen Bereich und im ebenfalls *bush* genannten Gebiet zwischen dem Küstenstreifen und dem Beginn des trockenen *Outback*,
- das Bild vom Eukalyptuswald ist typisch für die Baumvegetation,
- der gezeigte Regenwald kommt vor allem im Norden des Kontinents vor,
- die rote Sandwüste ist die vorherrschende Landschaftsformation des *Red Centre*, des Roten Herzens des *Outback*,
- das Foto vom *Great Barrier Reef* (mit einer Länge von ca. 2300 km das größte Korallenriff der Welt) steht stellvertretend für die den gesamten Kontinent umschließenden Ozeane.

Am Seitenrand werden vier Vögel vorgestellt, die man fast überall in diesem Land antreffen kann: der Lachende Hans (so genannt wegen seiner lauten keckernden Stimme), der Gelbhaubenkakadu (eine von 21 Arten von *Cockatoos* in Australien), der Ibis (der nicht nur in der freien Natur, sondern auch in den Großstädten heimisch ist) und der Emu (der gemeinsam mit dem Känguru das Wappentier Australiens ist).

Solutions

Activities p. 11

1. **Make a fact sheet of what you already know about Australia. Keep this record until you have finished the Australia course. Later, you can compare your knowledge about Down Under before and after you have completed this course.**
   Das Anfertigen einer Übersicht über das, was die Schüler schon vor dem Beginn des Kurses über Australien wussten, und der Vergleich mit dem Wissen nachher verschaffen ein Erfolgserlebnis und sind eine gute Motivation für die Behandlung weiterer Kursthemen.
   Zum Abschluss des Themas „Australia“ erhalten die Schüler die Gelegenheit, ihr Wissen in einem Quiz zu überprüfen (**s. Worksheet 10**).

2. **An easy way of keeping track of all your Australia reading and research is to keep a log book. This can be, for example, a 'Down Under Folder'. As you read this book and surf the Internet for information about Australia, write down facts and ideas to remember. As far as possible, collect photos and illustrations as well.**
   Die kontinuierliche Erfassung von Fakten und Wissen über ein Thema ist eine wichtige Verfahrensweise, die die Schüler auch auf andere Fächer und Wissensgebiete übertragen können. Die Lehrkraft sollte deshalb versuchen, gemeinsam mit der Klasse ein oder mehrere Verfahren (wie z. B. das log book) zur Dokumentation des Wissenszuwachses über Australien zu entwickeln.

3. **Page 9 shows two maps of Australia. The upper one has been created with south facing up. Stuart McArthur of Melbourne is said to have drawn it in 1973, at the age of 15, as an exchange student in Japan. He was sick of being taunted by his fellow students for coming 'from the bottom of the world'. Discuss this statement.**
   The other map is a regular political map showing the states and territories of the Commonwealth of Australia with their capitals.
   Complete these tasks:

a) **Count the number of states and territories of the Commonwealth.**
Six states and two territories:
- Australian Capital Territory (ACT) – Canberra (zugleich Hauptstadt des Commonwealth)
- New South Wales – Sydney
- Northern Territory – Darwin
- Queensland – Brisbane
- South Australia – Adelaide
- Tasmania – Hobart
- Victoria – Melbourne
- Western Australia – Perth

b) **First, speculate why the states and territories might have been given the names they have. Then search the web for exact information.**
- ACT is named after Canberra's role as the capital city of Australia since 1927.
- New South Wales was named by the British settlers after Wales in the United Kingdom.
- Queensland was named after Queen Elizabeth I.
- Tasmania got its name from the sea explorer Abel Tasman who also discovered New Zealand.
- Victoria was named after Queen Victoria.
- Northern Territory, South Australia and Western Australia have purely geographically-based names.

c) **Discuss some of the reasons why Australians might produce and sell such funny upside-down maps of 'Oz' and the world.**
Individual answers. The students should, however, point out that one of the most prominent reasons is the Australians' pride in their country, but also their commercial savvy.

d) **Locate the areas represented by the eight number plates shown on page 8.**
The students simply have to find the states and territories on the map and say which number plate belongs to each one.

4. **Brainstorm what the constituent parts of Australia's national flag and of its coat of arms (shown on p. 8) might mean. Prepare and give a five-minute talk about Australia and its national symbols.**
Australia's national flag consists of the British Union Jack in the top left corner and five stars representing the Southern Cross, which is a star formation that can be seen only in the southern hemisphere. The large white star on the left is known as the Commonwealth Star. Six points of the star represent the states while the seventh represents the territories.
The coat of arms also shows the Commonwealth Star. Below it, a red kangaroo and an emu, Australia's national animals, hold the shield with the badges of all states. These animals were chosen to symbolize a nation moving forward, as neither animal can move backwards easily.

5. **Search the web for some of the great men and women who attained fame and honour in Australia. Find out what they are famous for and give a short talk about each of them: Abel Tasman, James Cook, Arthur Phillip, Matthew Flinders, Lachlan Macquarie, John Macarthur, John McDouall Stuart, Harold Lasseter, Ludwig Leichhardt, Brettena Smyth.**
The students will consult various sources and report their findings about the different achievements of these ten people whose names are well-known in Australia. The following brief facts provide some background knowledge.

Abel Tasman (1603–1659): Tasman was a Dutch seafarer, explorer, and merchant. His crew was the first known European expedition to reach the islands of Van Diemen's Land (now Tasmania) and New Zealand in 1643.
James Cook (1728–1779): Cook was a British explorer, navigator and cartographer. He was the first known European to document the eastern coastline of Australia, exploring around the Great Barrier Reef in 1770.
Arthur Phillip (1738–1814): Phillip's father was German. Phillip was appointed captain of HMS Sirius and named Governor-Designate of New South Wales, the proposed British penal colony on the east coast of Australia.
Matthew Flinders (1774–1814): Flinders was one of the most successful navigators and cartographers of his age. He sailed with Captain William Bligh (cf. the film "Mutiny on the Bounty"), circumnavigated Australia and encouraged the use of that name for the continent.
Lachlan Macquarie (1762–1824): Macquarie was a British military officer and colonial administrator who served as Governor of New South Wales from 1810 to 1821 and played a leading role in the social, economic and architectural development of the colony. He is said to have had a big influence on the transition of New South Wales from a penal colony to a free settlement and therefore to have played a major role in the shaping of Australian society.
John Macarthur (1766–1834): Macarthur was a soldier, businessman, politician and pioneer in the Australian wool industry. He established Australia's first commercial winery and was one of the founding fathers of the Bank of Australia.
John McDouall Stuart (1815–1866): Stuart is probably the most famous of all Australia's early inland explorers. Stuart led the second expedition to traverse the Australian mainland from south to north, and was the first to do so from a starting point in South Australia; his explorations eventually resulted in the Adelaide-Darwin telegraph being built and the main route from Port Augusta to Darwin being established, which is now known as the Stuart Highway in his honour.
Harold Lasseter (1880–1931): Lasseter travelled a lot in both Australia and the United States. As a young man, he claimed to have discovered a fabulously rich gold reef ("Lasseter's Reef") in central Australia; however, he died trying to find it again and all further attempts have been equally unsuccessful; the road from Stuart Highway is named after him ("Lasseter Highway").
Ludwig Leichhardt (1813–ca. 1848): Leichhardt was a German explorer and naturalist; his last expedition was the inspiration for the novel "Voss" by Patrick White; the Inner Western Sydney suburb of Leichhardt and the surrounding Municipality of Leichhardt are named after him, as is the Leichhardt Highway in Queensland.
Brettena Smyth (1840?–1898): As a widowed mother of four children, Brettena Smyth ran a drapery and druggist's shop, which became a landmark in the struggle for women's rights; the shop was the venue for meetings of the Australian Women's Suffrage Society in the 1880s and 1890s.

6. **Describe the landscape pictures on page 10. Then continue the Prime Minister's statement. Give at least three examples in which you try to prove that the geography has indeed "contributed to developing the Australian character".**
Up to now, the students have not learned a lot about Australia. They therefore will have to guess that the country's diverse landscapes must have brought about people of very different characters. What they do know is that the continent is surrounded by oceans and has several climatically very different vegetational zones (a densely-populated coastline with beaches and cliffs, green farmland, rainforests, hot and dry deserts in which almost only Aborigines can survive). Accordingly, the students might, for example, answer that

- over thousands of years, Indigenous people have been living across this vast country and have successfully adapted to its extreme climatical conditions,
- Australians (above all, the descendants of the British and other European conquerors) have become a nation that loves beaches and the ocean, although also having to struggle with its dangers. This is most probably because a great deal of their roughly 200-years-old "white" history was written by explorers, navigators and cartographers who had come by ship and because the vast majority of the population live at or near the coast,
- in the 19th/20th centuries, people of different professions did their best to conquer the diverse landscapes of Australia. Their characters were shaped in the process of harnessing the power and dealing with hazards of Mother Nature and as a result of adapting to the various natural conditions they were faced with (explorers, pioneers, stockmen on cattle stations, swagmen, winegrowers, wool mill owners, gold diggers, miners, and many others).

Auf der Seite 11 ist außerdem die Nationalflagge Australiens abgebildet, anhand derer im Unterrichtsgespräch die Bedeutung der einzelnen Bestandteile der Flagge herausgearbeitet werden.

Young People in Australia

Die Texte dieses Kapitels sind zusammengestellt nach verschiedenen Webseiten, hauptsächlich www.youthweek.com. Es geht hierbei um die größte Veranstaltung für Jugendliche in Australien, in die seit dem Jahr 2000 jährlich mehrere zehntausend Kinder und Jugendliche einbezogen sind. Das Kapitel wird aufgrund seines altersgemäßen Inhalts von Interesse sein und gibt Anregungen für eigene Veranstaltungen und Wettbewerbe.

National Youth Week

Auf den Seiten 12 und 13 werden die einzelnen Wettbewerbe und die allgemeinen Voraussetzungen für die Teilnahme beschrieben sowie die Preise ausgelobt. Die Illustrationen an den Seitenrändern zeigen Jugendliche in den Großstädten Australiens in der Freizeit und beim Studium.

I never knew this about Australia

Da jedes Jahr neue Sieger in den verschiedenen Wettbewerben zur *National Youth Week* ermittelt werden, kann die Information in dieser Box nur den Stand zu Redaktionsschluss des Schülerbuchs widerspiegeln.
Darum wird stattdessen die indigene Jugendliche Tania Major als *Young Australian of the Year 2007* vorgestellt. Sie ist eine von den *Aborigines*, die sich in der australischen Gesellschaft durch besondere Leistungen hervortun. Ausführlich zur Auszeichnung *Young Australian of the Year* siehe: www.australianoftheyear.org.au
Zu beiden Themen kann die Klasse selbstständig weiter recherchieren.

Solutions

Activities p. 13

1. **Which competitions does National Youth Week comprise? What are their potential participants invited to create?**
   RockIT – write and record an original piece of rock music
   WriteIT – compose a piece of creative writing
   ShootIT – shoot a short film about a young person's life
   DesignIT – create a digital static design
   SnapIT – take a photo on the theme "Action and adventure in the outdoors"
   The students should, of course, give a little more information than this. In particular, they should be able to describe the tasks in more detail. Additionally, they could also speak about the prizes offered as an incentive.
2. **If you had the chance to take part in NYW, which of the competitions would you take part in? Give reasons for your decision.**
   Individual answers.
3. **Do similar competitions exist in Germany? Would you like to have them in your area, too? Discuss.**
   The students might think of and describe events such as Weltjugendtag, Bundeswettbewerbe (Fremdsprachen, Musik, Naturwissenschaften), or any other local competitions and events.

4. **Make five posters that might attract young people's interest. Give your posters eye-catching headlines, such as 'Get involved', 'Be in the running for cool prizes', or 'Be creative'.**
The class is asked to make five posters in smaller groups. Alternatively, the teacher could offer the students the option of making just one poster together or working on it in a special afternoon group.

5. **Find out more about Tania Major, and why she has become a role model for young Australians, and about Ms Jonty Bush, the award winner for 2009. Who is the current Young Australian of the Year?**
This is a websearch task that the students could do in the English classroom, in special IT rooms or at home.
Tania Major, an Indigenous youth advocate, has become a role model for all young Australians because she has managed, as an Aboriginal girl, to complete a university degree and to speak out on TV about a number of issues concerning the welfare of young Indigenous people. See http://www.australianoftheyear.org.au/pages/page310.asp.

> "Tania Major came to public attention three years ago as the youngest person ever elected to ATSIC (The Aboriginal and Torres Strait Islander Commission). She broke the ice of public discussion about a number of issues concerning the welfare of young Indigenous people when she was featured on national television programs such as *Four Corners* and *60 Minutes*. She made some people feel very uncomfortable, and was happy to do so. She spoke directly and very publicly to the prime minister and other opinion leaders about the appalling secrets of domestic violence in her community in the belief that the best way to represent her people was to tell the truth. So far, Tania is the only person within her community to have completed a university degree; indeed, she's the only one to have successfully completed Year 12. Tania has become a role model not only for Indigenous youth, but also for all young Australians."

The Young Australian of the Year award has been awarded since 1979 to recognize outstanding and exceptional Australians aged 16 to 30. Young Australian of the Year 2009 was Jonty Bush. She has dedicated her award to the victims of crime she helps everyday. See http://www.australianoftheyear.org.au
The Australian of the Year award was introduced in 1960 to celebrate outstanding Australians. To honour recipients, the Australians of the Year Walk was created in Canberra, which consists of one hundred concrete pillars with their names and pictures. See http://en.wikipedia.org/wiki/Australian_of_the_Year.

6. **Imagine German local authorities want you to inform them about NYW. Mediate the text. You need not translate literally into German.**
Example:
Seit dem Jahr 2000 gibt es in Australien die National Youth Week, die Nationale Jugendwoche. An ihr nehmen alljährlich hunderttausende Kinder und Jugendliche aus dem ganzen Land teil. Die Hauptziele bestehen darin, den Ideenreichtum der Teilnehmer bekannt zu machen, ihre Talente zu fördern, ihnen eine Gelegenheit zu verschaffen, in der Öffentlichkeit aufzutreten und einfach Spaß zu haben. Die Teilnehmer kommen von Schulen, Universitäten und Berufsschuleinrichtungen. An der Organisation der vielen Veranstaltungen beteiligen sich außer den Jugendverbänden staatliche und kommunale Behörden, Firmen und andere Sponsoren.
In dieser Woche finden hunderte von Veranstaltungen statt: Sportwettkämpfe, Tanzpartys, kommunale Projekte, Konferenzen, Debatten, Ausstellungen, Festivals, Foren und Livekonzerte.

Der Wettbewerbsteil umfasst fünf Sparten: Musik, kreatives Schreiben, Film, Design und Fotografie. Die Gewinner erhalten wertvolle Preise, ihre Namen werden im Internet veröffentlicht.

Celebrate Being a Young Australian

Anknüpfend an die vorangegangenen Texte ist hier im ersten Text nachzulesen, welche Bedeutung die gesamtaustralische Regierung dieser großen Jugendveranstaltung beimisst. Der Textausschnitt stammt aus der Botschaft von Kate Ellis, der Ministerin für Jugendfragen, die selbst noch recht jugendlich ist (geboren 1977), anlässlich der *National Youth Week* 2008.

Im unteren Teil der Seite 14 wird im Text die *National Youth Week 2008* beschrieben. Herausragend ist angesichts der relativ geringen Einwohnerzahl Australiens die hohe Teilnehmerzahl von fast 300 000 Jugendlichen. Dieser Text kann den Schülern als Muster für eine eigene Beschreibung der Jugendwoche in dem Jahr dienen, in dem sie dieses Kursthema behandeln.

Der Text wird umrahmt von Logos einiger Sponsoren und Partner der *National Youth Week*. Die Aufgabe dazu wird in den *Activities* gestellt.

Talent Comps – 2008 Winners

Auf der Seite 15 werden die Sieger von vier Wettbewerben vorgestellt. Die Abbildungen am Seitenrand zeigen zwei der Objekte, die einen Preis erhielten. Die Preisträger jedes Jahres sind in einer Internetrecherche unter www.youthweek.com zu finden.

Solutions

Activities p. 16

1. **Work in pairs.**
   a) **Choose one of the labels of NYW sponsors and partners on p. 14, and then surf the Internet for more information about it. What do the labels tell you about Australia? Give a short talk on your topic.**
   Generally speaking, the labels make it clear that many institutions and companies support the National Youth Week as organizers and sponsors. This shows that NYW is an event of great national importance.
   These are the main sponsoring and supporting institutions and companies and their websites.
   Sponsors:
   Commonwealth Bank Foundation – www.commbank.com.au/
   Beyond Blue – www.beyondblue.org.au/
   Scouts Australia – www.scouts.com.au/
   Australian Federal Police – www.afp.gov.au
   Partners:
   Network Ten – http://ten.com.au/
   Pop Republic – www.poprepublic.com
   SBS – www.sbs.com.au/
   Joy 94.9 FM – www.joy.org.au/
   Imparja Television – www.imparja.com/
   Inspire Foundation – www.inspire.org.au/
   Allans Music – www.allansmusic.com.au/
   Vibewire.net – http://vibewire.org/

b) **Search the web for information about the bands and singers mentioned on p. 14. Introduce them to the class.**
The Presets: The Presets are a dance punk duo from Sydney, consisting of Julian Hamilton and Kim Moyes. Their debut album "Beams" was released in 2005. (www.thepresets.com/deterioration_content.html)
Operator Please: Operator Please is a baroque pop band of five musicians formed in 2005 in Queensland. (www.operatorpleaseband.com)
Delta Goodrem: Delta Lea Goodrem is an Australian singer, songwriter, and actress. She starred in the popular soap "Neighbours" as Nina Tucker. She makes pop and adult contemporary music. (www.deltagoodrem.com)
Brian McFadden: Brian McFadden is an Irish singer and songwriter who became famous in Australia through his engagement to the pop star Delta Goodrem (www.brianmcfadden.com.au)
The students' presentations should not exceed five minutes. They can, however, include short examples of music.

2. **What hopes and plans for the future do the four young Aussies have? Are they similar to yours? Draw up mindmaps and compare.**
   - Nikki Malvar currently has a crisis of occupational aspiration, although she is highly talented.
   - Mark Sebastian wants to make videos and has already published several popular YouTube videos.
   - Rhiana Chan hopes to be a graphic designer one day.
   - Tom Stanford wants to be a professional photographer.

   The answers to the second question may vary.
   The mindmaps could also be drawn on the blackboard.

3. **Two of the short biographies are told in the first person, the other two in the third person. Are there any differences as to their effectiveness? Which perspective do you like more? Why? Discuss.**
   When a biography is told in the first person, it sounds very authentic. The reader feels closer to the writer than in the case of third-person narratives. Naturally, it depends on the readers which perspective they like best.

Sydney – Capital of the Young

In diesem Buch werden die beiden größten Städte Australiens, Sydney und Melbourne, gesondert vorgestellt. Die Fotos auf der Seite 17 zeigen einige der vielen in Sydney möglichen Freizeitbeschäftigungen von Jugendlichen. Sie sollen kurz beschrieben und besprochen werden, können jedoch auch z. B. zu weiterführenden Recherchen über die einzelnen Lokalitäten benutzt werden.

Pictures

The pictures from top left to bottom right:
The Strand Arcade was built in 1891 and is the last remaining one of formerly five large shopping centres in Sydney built in the 19th century. It is a great place to meet in good cafés and do exclusive shopping.
The Sydney Opera House is the largest opera house in Australia. It was built between 1957 and 1973 according to a design by the Danish architect Jørn Utzon. The area around it is a favourite meeting place for young people and tourists.
The next photo shows the **Central Business District** as seen from Darling Harbour. In the foreground, you can see the Sydney Monorail opened in 1988, which connects Darling Harbour, Chinatown and the Sydney central business and shopping districts.

The Domain is Sydney's largest public park. Here everybody can relax, do sports or have a barbecue (or, in Australian slang, a barbie).
Diving at Manly Beach is one of dozens of sports activities Australians love to do.
Luna Park is located north of Sydney Harbour, directly at the northern end of Harbour Bridge. The amusement park was opened in 1935 and still is an attraction for young and old.

Weitere Möglichkeiten der Freizeitbeschäftigung können zum Beispiel der Taronga Zoo und der Royal Botanical Garden bieten. Alle Bilder sollten zunächst beschrieben und dann auf ihren Inhalt hin diskutiert werden. Nicht gezeigt, aber selbstverständlich vorhanden, sind zahlreiche Kinos und Discos. Aber auch ohne diesen Hinweis wird die Kursgruppe viele Anhaltspunkte dafür finden, wie junge Leute in Sydney ihre Zeit verbringen können.

Living in Australia

In diesem Kapitel werden Streiflichter auf das Leben in Australien geworfen. Anhand von Zeitungsausschnitten, deren Thematik so gewählt wurde, dass sie die Interessen der Schüler in der Oberstufe tangieren, werden Menschen und Lebenssituationen vorgestellt: *Immigration and Australian values, IT in Australia, Sports, Living in a megacity (Melbourne), IT in school, Studying and living in Australia* und *Education deficit*. Es ist zu empfehlen, die Texte entweder auf einzelne Schüler oder auf Schülergruppen aufzuteilen und dann ihre Inhalte vortragen zu lassen. Jedes Thema ist exemplarisch und lässt sich durch weitere Recherchen und Diskussionen erweitern. Vorschläge dazu enthalten die *Activities*.

News around Australia

Der Textteil wird eingeleitet mit einem Zitat von Bill Bryson aus seinem Australienbuch „Down Under". Dieses unterhaltsam geschriebene Reisebuch ist sehr vergnüglich zu lesen und enthält eine Vielzahl von Passagen, die entweder im Unterricht gelesen oder der Klasse als häusliche Aufgabe übertragen werden können. Bei der Bestellung dieses Buchs sollte beachtet werden, dass es sowohl in amerikanischem als auch in britischem Englisch erhältlich ist.
Die Zeitungsartikel werden durch einige Illustrationen aus den jeweiligen Medien ergänzt. Das Foto auf Seite 18 zeigt, wie die Teilnehmer an einem Jugendparlament in Melbourne vehement auf die in den nächsten Tagen vor ihnen stehenden Aufgaben eingestimmt werden: Die im Vordergrund zu sehenden Organisatoren sprechen laut und mit viel Mimik und Gestik mitreißende Losungen vor, die die auf der Freitreppe stehende Gruppe laut wiederholt. Das Bild auf Seite 19 gehört zum abgedruckten Zeitungsartikel und lässt die Begeisterung während des Empfangs der Olympioniken von Peking 2008 in Sydney erahnen. Die beiden Fotos auf Seite 20 zeigen das aus England nach Melbourne gebrachte Geburtshaus von James Cook, das als Museum eingerichtet ist, sowie geschäftige Passanten aus Banken und Büros in der Mittagspause. Das Bild zu Text 7 auf Seite 21 wurde in einem Hotel aufgenommen und demonstriert die im Text kritisierten Probleme mit der englischen Sprache (Schreibung „*know*" anstelle von „*now*"). Dieses Beispiel der orthografischen (und anderen) Schwierigkeiten, die auch mancher *native speaker* mit seiner englischen Muttersprache hat, dient Lernern angesichts ihrer eigenen Probleme häufig als Beruhigung, kann aber auch motivieren zu weiterem intensiven Bemühen um gute Sprachkompetenz.

I never knew this about Australia

Die hier zusammengetragenen Daten halten Hintergrundinformationen zu den sieben Zeitungsausschnitten bereit. Sie sollten von der ganzen Klasse gelesen und nach Möglichkeit in den jeweils zu referierenden Artikel einbezogen werden. Außerdem bieten sich auch hier weiterführende Recherchen an, zum Beispiel zur Immigration, zu den australischen Werten, zur Bevölkerungsexplosion in Sydney und Melbourne, zum Schulsystem, zum Freizeit- und Leistungssport oder zum Studium in Australien. Zum letzteren Thema ein Zitat aus der Zeitschrift „Stern": „1996 waren deutsche Studenten in Australien noch echte Exoten auf dem Campus – nicht einmal 200 von ihnen verirrten sich dorthin. Im Jahr 2005 tummelten sich schon knapp 2800 in den Hörsälen zwischen Perth und Sydney. Hochschulbildung ist in Australien inzwischen neben Tou-

rismus zu einem der zentralen Wirtschaftszweige aufgestiegen." (Markus Wanzeck: „Deutsche Studenten gehen fremd", www.stern.de, 14.09.2007 [12.04.2010])
Das Thema „Sport" wird durch eine Fotografie von Catherine Freeman, der ersten indigenen Goldmedaillengewinnerin bei den Olympischen Spielen 2000, und durch einen Schnappschuss von sportlicher Freizeitbeschäftigung in Sydney illustriert. Die Großstadtthematik wird untermalt durch zwei Bilder aus Sydney: die Sydney Harbour Bridge und eine multinationale Schulklasse beim Museumsbesuch.
Zum Thema „Moderne Schule" (letzter Anführungspunkt) können Details nachgelesen werden unter: www.abc.net.au/news/stories/2008/08/20/2341657.htm.

Solutions

Activities p. 23

1. **What do these texts tell you about Australia? Give a summary of each of them. In your summaries, include the information given in the box on p. 22.**
   Individual answers.
   The teacher may let the students choose the articles or distribute them herself or himself.

2. **Search the web addresses provided or surf other sites for further details about the issues dealt with in texts 1 to 7, and then present and discuss the topics.**
   1) **Ahmed Fahour describes his and his parents' good experiences as immigrants to Australia. How might immigrants to Germany sum up their feelings? (www.immi.gov.au/media/fact-sheets)**
      The answers may vary, depending on where the students live. However, they should take into account that there are always positive and negative feelings such as (positive:) living in a free, democratic country, having new chances to earn one's living, or (negative:) homesickness, having no job, experiencing problems with Germans or other immigrant nations, etc.
   2) **What do you learn from this text about Australia's scientific skills? (www.anu.edu.au/discoveranu/content/podcasts/itc_industry)**
      Australia is not a poor or underdeveloped country at all (as the term "Down Under" itself might suggest), but a highly-developed country with a strong IT industry. Many processes are completely controlled by computers, so that hackers can be a big problem as they are in the USA or Germany.
   3) **The third article is about Sydney's triumphant welcome to Australian Olympians. Australian athletes rank top five in the world. In which disciplines? Which sports stars do you know? (www.athletics.com.au, www.paralympic.org.au)**
      The students' answers will vary as the sports scene does from year to year. However, there are some general facts that can be stated.
      "Australia has more than 120 national sporting organisations and thousands of state, regional and club bodies. It is estimated that about a third of the population are registered sports participants. Many more are involved in activities such as fishing, bushwalking, recreational boating, horse riding and fitness programs. Water sports have a huge following and the high interest in sailing is reflected in Australia's entry in every America's Cup challenge since 1967. In September 1983, Australia II became the first foreign yacht to win the cup that had been held by the U.S. since 1851." (from: http://www.totaltravel.com.au/library/traveller/aussiesports)
      Rugby, cricket, golf, soccer, rowing, sailing, tennis, cycling, swimming, athletics belong to Australia's top sports. Australian athletes rank among the best in the world in these disciplines.

Some of the most famous sportsmen and sportswomen from Australia are: Rod Laver (tennis), Catherine Freeman (athletics), Ricky Ponting (cricket), Geoff Ogilvy (golf), Ian Thorpe (swimming), Lleyton Hewitt (tennis).

4) **Does Bernard Salt want to live in a city of six million or more residents? Would you? Discuss some of the pros and cons of living in a megacity. (www.tinyurl.com/m52wht)**
   Bernard Salt says, "You don't have to live in Melbourne." Nevertheless, he loves living there, but would not want to live in a megacity of millions and millions of people. He does not want Melbourne to grow into an uncontrollable and uncomfortable urban monster.
   The answers as to the pros and cons of living in a megacity may vary.
5) **Search the web for more information about IT in Australia's schools and compare it to your school. (www.tinyurl.com/lktg9c)**
   "The bandwidth available to schools varies between states and territories. Different schools have access to connections that vary in speed from dial-up modem, through ISDN (the most common form of connection), to ADSL and in some rare instances, cable and satellite. In most states and territories, the majority of schools have either 64 kbps or 128 kbps ISDN lines. In Western Australia, the majority of schools currently have 64 kbps dial on-demand Internet connections while schools in the Northern Territory have 400 kbps satellite connections." (Extract from the website given above.)
   In April 2009, the Australian government launched an ambitious plan to make Australia one of the world's most wired countries in a project to extend broadband Internet access across the country. In accordance with this plan, a new state-controlled company will build a A$ 43 billion network. Announcing the plan, Prime Minister Kevin Rudd said it would deliver broadband speeds of 100 megabits per second to 90% of Australian homes, schools and businesses within eight years through fibre-optic cables. The other 10% would get a wireless upgrade.
6) **Andrew Stevenson writes about a Canadian woman who moved to Australia to study and work here. Can you imagine studying Down Under? (http://studyinaustralia.gov.au)**
   Individual answers.
7) **Do German students have similar problems with their native language? What is the VCE equivalent to in Germany? (https://aei.gov.au/AEI/CEP/Australia/EducationSystem/default.htm)**
   Obviously, there are people all around the world who have problems with their mother tongue, So it is natural that some German students do as well. The question is how they manage to cope with these problems. One of the results of the class discussion could be that the students should recognize the importance of learning not only English, but also German, as well as possible.
   The VCE is equivalent to the German Abitur.

3. **Search newspapers like 'The Age', 'The Australian', or 'The Sunday Telegraph' for more everyday events in Australia. You might simply decide to read any article you are interested in, or choose a particular topic of interest you want to look at more closely.**
   Reading Australian newspapers can easily be done on the Internet. In larger towns, Australian newspapers can also be bought in kiosks and bookshops. Alternatively, the class could contact the Australian Embassy in Berlin and ask them to send a number of old copies.

The students should feel free to choose topics based on their interests. Their presentations should not exceed five minutes though, so that as many students as possible get the chance to speak to the class.

4. **Which song is the official national anthem of the Commonwealth of Australia? Find an audio version of Australia's anthem on the Internet, and listen to it. First, read and translate the lyrics, and then discuss the message of the song.**
Australia's official National Anthem is "Advance Australia Fair". The main message of this song is for all Australians to show and support their national pride in their history and to encourage them to stand together and make the Commonwealth of Australia a strong and renowned country in the world. (see **Worksheet 1**). The patriotic song was written by Peter Dodds McCormick, a first-generation immigrant from Scotland, and first sung in 1878. (Audio version with pictures: http://www.youtube.com/watch?v=6iGNhgMd6uM)
In 1984, Australia's former national anthem "God Save the Queen", was designated from then on as the Royal Anthem to be played at public engagements in Australia attended by members of the Royal family, and 'Advance Australia Fair' was finally declared to be the official Australian national anthem. Today, Australians sing a revised version of just two of its stanzas. Nevertheless, it is often joked that many Australians do not even know the first, largely as a small act of rebellion against the choice of this song rather than the more popular "Waltzing Matilda", which is considered by many to be the unofficial and preferred national anthem of Australia.

5. **Another very popular national song is "I am Australian", written by Bruce Woodley and Dobe Newton in 1987. It was, for example, sung during the Australian National Mourning Service for the victims of the 2009 Black Saturday bush fires. Search the web for the lyrics of this song and discuss why it might have become so dear to the 'Aussies'.**
"I am Australian" has become so popular because the song presents Australians and their national pride in simple and comprehensible words.

Worksheet 1

Australia's National Anthem "Advance Australia Fair"

Translation

Australians all let us rejoice,
For we are young and free;
We've golden soil and wealth for toil;
Our home is girt by sea;
Our land abounds in nature's gifts
Of beauty rich and rare;
In history's page, let every stage
Advance Australia Fair.

In joyful strains then let us sing,
Advance Australia Fair.
Beneath our radiant Southern Cross
We'll toil with hearts and hands;
To make this Commonwealth of ours
Renowned of all the lands;
For those who've come across the seas
We've boundless plains to share;
With courage let us all combine
To Advance Australia Fair.
In joyful strains then let us sing,
Advance Australia Fair.

Worksheet 1 Solution

Australia's National Anthem "Advance Australia Fair"

Australians all let us rejoice,
For we are young and free;
We've golden soil and wealth for toil;
Our home is girt by sea;
Our land abounds in nature's gifts
Of beauty rich and rare;
In history's page, let every stage
Advance Australia Fair.
In joyful strains then let us sing,
Advance Australia Fair.

Beneath our radiant Southern Cross
We'll toil with hearts and hands;
To make this Commonwealth of ours
Renowned of all the lands;
For those who've come across the seas
We've boundless plains to share;
With courage let us all combine
To Advance Australia Fair.
In joyful strains then let us sing,
Advance Australia Fair.

Beispielübersetzung

Australier alle, lasst uns jubeln,
Denn wir sind jung und frei;
Wir haben goldnen Boden und durch Arbeit geht's uns gut;
Unsre Heimat ist umgürtet von Meeren;
Unser Land ist reich an natürlichen Gaben
Voll Schönheit, reich und rar;
Auf den Seiten unsrer Geschichte lasst in jeder Phase
Australien aufblühen.
Alsdann in frohen Weisen lasst uns singen,
Australien blühe auf.

Unter unserem strahlenden Kreuz des Südens
Packen wir an mit Herz und Hand;
Um diesen unsern Staatenbund
Berühmt zu machen in allen Ländern;
Mit denen, die von Übersee gekommen,
Haben wir endlose Weiten zu teilen;
Mit Mut lasst uns all zusammenstehen,
Damit Australien aufblüht.
Alsdann in frohen Weisen lasst uns singen,
Australien blühe auf.

Australian Culture

Die australische Kultur ruht vor allem auf zwei Säulen: der Kultur der Urbevölkerung und der Kultur der britischen und anderen europäischen Entdecker, Siedler und Einwanderer. Hinzu gesellen sich die in der zweiten Hälfte des 20. Jahrhunderts allmählich dominant werdenden kulturellen Einflüsse der Immigranten aus anderen Teilen der Welt, vor allen Dingen aber aus Asien. Das Kapitel „Australian Culture" macht die Schüler bekannt mit einigen Elementen der indigenen Kultur der Vergangenheit und Gegenwart, mit dem Song „Waltzing Matilda", der „heimlichen Hymne" der Australier, und einigen Beispielen der modernen bildenden Kunst und Literatur sowie aus Film und Fernsehen.

Je nach den Interessen der Lerner können die gewünschten Themen und Texte gelesen und bearbeitet werden. Jeder Text eröffnet auch die Möglichkeit weiterer Recherchen. Die Verständniskontrolle kann auf verschiedenen Wegen erfolgen: in Schülerpräsentationen, mithilfe von Postern oder in Unterrichtsgesprächen.

Eine unterhaltsame und zugleich interessante Ergänzung zum Thema „Australische Kultur" im Unterricht oder als häusliche Arbeit kann die Webseite www.convictcreations.com/culture/index.htm sein, auf der eine Vielzahl von unterhaltsamen und interessanten „*unusual Australian facts*" zusammengetragen wurde.

Aboriginal Art

Die Spuren indigenen Kunstschaffens begegnen dem Australienreisenden überall. In den letzten Jahrzehnten haben sich viele Künstlergruppen nur aus *Aborigines* oder gemeinsam mit Künstlern anderer Nationalitäten gebildet, die im In- und Ausland teilweise große Bedeutung erlangten. Auf der Seite 24 wird der indigene Maler Harry Tjutjuna vorgestellt, der einer solchen Gruppe in der Missionsschule von Ernabella im südlichen Outback angehört. Die drei Bilder auf dieser Seite verdeutlichen die allgegenwärtige Präsenz des Kunstschaffens der Aborigines.

Im Internet sind unzählige Seiten über die Kunst der indigenen Völker Australiens zu finden. Auf der kommerziellen Seite www.aboriginalartdirectory.com werden zum Beispiel sehr viele Fotos gezeigt, die geeignet sind, sich eine etwas umfassendere Vorstellung von der australischen indigenen Kunst zu verschaffen. Speziell Ernabella Arts und Harry Tjutjuna werden auf der Seite www.aboriginalartdirectory.com/shop/aboriginal-art-centre/ernabella-arts-inc.php vorgestellt.

Solutions

Activities p. 24

1. **What subjects do artists like Harry Tjutjuna concentrate on?**
   Typically, Aboriginal artists focus their work on ancient, traditional themes and motifs such as the use of Aboriginal pictographs, mythological symbols, animal pictures, and other rich ornamentation. Many of the younger contemporary artists, however, also create works that convey political and social messages.

2. **Describe the examples of Aboriginal art which can be found everywhere in Australia. What are their characteristic features?**
   The students should describe what they see in the pictures on p. 24, or find any other piece of Aboriginal art, and describe it.

The picture at the top just shows a number of circles painted on a stone. This is an ancient Aboriginal symbol for a meeting place.
The central picture is painted on a litter bin. In this picture, circles are used as well. Furthermore, we recognize the typical technique of creating rich ornamentation by using many dots of different colours (this is the so-called Aboriginal dot painting technique). The upper pictures in the black circles seem to show fruits, the blue wave might be a river, the hoof-shaped signs with straight lines next to them on the right and at the bottom of the picture represent men with their spears.
The third photo was taken in the main airport building of Alice Springs. Here, the carpet on the floor is richly decorated with Aboriginal art. The ornament at the bottom is obviously the sun; to the right of it, we recognize a river; in the right corner at the bottom, we see two waves and water drops in between representing rain; to the right and left of the river, there are the signs of Aboriginal men.
For more detailed information about dot painting, see http://www.ohmsartgallery.com/aboriganal.htm.

3. **Search the web for more information about Aboriginal art. Prepare a multimedia presentation on this issue.**
   Individual answers. The students' multimedia presentation may include, for example, the use of photos, books, the PC, or a PowerPoint presentation.

Aboriginal Music

Dieses Thema wird die besondere Aufmerksamkeit der Lerner erwecken, weil es um ein Musikgenre geht, das zumindest einige von ihnen kennen oder schätzen. Die Gruppe *Yothu Yindi* ist international bekannt. Indigene und europäische Musiker vereinigen bodenständige indigene Musik mit westlicher Pop- und Rockmusik. Das findet seinen Niederschlag auch in der gemischten Instrumentation. Neben urtümlichen australischen Instrumenten (*Didgeridoo* und *Bilma*) stehen moderne westliche Instrumente. Bei der Arbeit mit diesem Text können insbesondere jene Schüler einbezogen werden, die Musik gern aus dem Netz herunterladen und vorspielen wollen. Denn dieses Thema sollte nicht ohne akustische Beispiele behandelt werden.
Aktuell treten immer wieder neue indigene Künstler aus Australien in Erscheinung. Im Juli 2009 war es zum Beispiel der blinde Sänger und Multiinstrumentalist (Gitarre, Schlagzeug, Keybord und *Yidaki*) *Geoffrey Gurrumul Yunupingu*, der zehn Jahre lang der Gruppe *Yothu Yindi* angehörte, aber erst in den ersten Jahren des 21. Jahrhunderts als Solist weltweit berühmt wurde und auch in Europas Städten grandiose Erfolge einspielte. (Musikbeispiele und mehr Informationen siehe www.gurrumul.com).

Solutions

Activities p. 25

1. **What kind of music does Yothu Yindi produce? What instruments do its members play?**
   Yothu Yindi produces traditional Aboriginal music combined with western rock and pop. In their songs, they often refer to Australia's fauna and landscapes.
   Along with modern western musical instruments, the group uses a number of Aboriginal instruments, for example, different kinds of yidaki (didgeridoos) and bilmas (indigenous clapping sticks).

2. **Go to www.yothuyindi.com. Close your eyes and listen to Yothu Yindi's music. What visions come to your mind? Discuss.**

Individual answers. Learning about other people's culture and listening to their music offers a good chance for the teacher to create short periods of silence and relaxation in the English classroom lesson.

3. **Read between the lines. What does the last paragraph of the text tell you about the band's political activity, and what do you conclude from this about the place of indigenous people in Australian society?**
The last paragraph of the text says: "The band recorded their first album *Homeland Movement* in Australia's bicentennial year, 1988. Yothu Yindi performed bicentennial protest concerts in Sydney, headlined the first Festival of Aboriginal Rock Music in Darwin (later appearing in the television documentary *Sing Loud Play Strong*) and embarked on a 32-date tour of the United States and Canada with Australia's most politicised rockers Midnight Oil. Also that year, the band's founding member and lead singer, Mandawuy Yunupingu, became the first Aboriginal person from Arnhem Land to gain a tertiary degree when he graduated with a Bachelor of Arts (Education) from Deakin University."
This paragraph tells us that Yothu Yindi were engaged in political activities with their music (protest concerts in Sydney in 1988, U.S. and Canadian concerts together with political activists Midnight Oil).
From this, the students can draw the conclusion that even today there are still problems that indigenous people in Australia have to face, but that more and more of them are taking on the role of political and educational activists or using the chance to get a higher education.

Waltzing Matilda

A. B. Paterson

Der bekannteste australische *folk song* sollte möglichst wenig durch Interpretation oder sprachliche Diskussion „zerredet" werden. Das Wichtigste ist der emotionale Eindruck, den das Anhören des Songs hinterlässt (s. den Link unten). Das Lied lässt eine für europäische Ohren heute vielleicht ungewohnte anheimelnde Lagerfeuerromantik entstehen und wird von den Australiern zu vielen Gelegenheiten, z. B. auch anlässlich eines Barbecues, angestimmt.
Zur Vermittlung der neuen Vokabeln dient die kleine Übung auf Seite 26, bei der es darum geht, die kleingeschriebenen Wörter aus der akustischen Videoversion zu entnehmen. Ein Wort (*billabong*) wird durch ein Foto auf dem Seitenrand illustriert, der *swagman* durch die Zeichnung. Wenn die Möglichkeit der akustischen Erschließung des Liedtextes nicht besteht oder die Lehrkraft aus bestimmten Gründen anders vorgehen möchte, können die einzusetzenden Worte auch schon an der Tafel vorgegeben und nur der richtigen Stelle zugeordnet werden: (in alphabetischer Reihenfolge) *billabong, billy, coolibah, glee, jumbuck, squatter, swagman, thoroughbred, troopers, tucker bag.*
Die Vermittlung der neuen Vokabeln dient nicht in erster Linie der Erweiterung des Wortschatzes. Sie sollen vor allem angeeignet werden, um den Liedtext zu verstehen und seinen Inhalt auf Englisch wiederzugeben.
Nicht minder bedeutsam ist es, den Schülern die Einsicht zu vermitteln, dass im australischen Englisch sehr viele Lexeme existieren, die es in anderen regionalen Registern nicht gibt, ganz besonders viele naturgemäß aus den Sprachen der Ureinwohner. Um sich einen Eindruck vom australischen Slang (dem sogenannten *strine*) zu verschaffen, ist z. B. die Webseite http://goaustralia.about.com/cs/language/a/strinea.htm geeignet.

Solutions

1. **Read and translate the song, then look for it on www.youtube.com and listen to it. While listening, substitute the original words for the words and phrases printed in small letters.**
There are many different versions of "Waltzing Matilda". In this book, the song text follows the generally-accepted version. For a variation see www.matildacentre.com.au and many other websites.

Activities p. 26

> Once a jolly swagman camped by a billabong,
> Under the shade of a coolibah tree.
> And he sang as he watched and waited till his billy boiled,
> 'Who'll come a-waltzing Matilda with me?'
>
> Chorus: 'Waltzing Matilda, waltzing Matilda,
> You'll come a-waltzing Matilda with me.'
>
> Down came a jumbuck to drink at the billabong.
> Up jumped the swagman and grabbed him with glee
> And he sang as he put that jumbuck in his tucker bag,
> 'You'll come a-waltzing Matilda with me!' – Chorus
>
> Up came the squatter riding on his thoroughbred.
> Up came the troopers, one, two, three.
> 'Whose is that jolly jumbuck you've got in your tucker bag?
> You'll come a-waltzing Matilda with me!' – Chorus
>
> Up jumped the swagman and sprang into the billabong.
> 'You'll never catch me alive!' said he.
> And his ghost may be heard as you pass by that billabong,
> 'Who'll come a-waltzing Matilda with me?' – Chorus

2. **Learn the new words and retell the song in your own words.**
Apart from the words listed above, the following words could also be new: jolly, to grab. Content of the song:
One day, a swagman was camping by a billabong in the Outback. He was singing a song and waiting for his billy to boil. When he saw a jumbuck drinking water at the billabong, he caught and slaughtered it, and stowed it away in his tucker bag. Suddenly, the squatter and some policemen came and wanted to arrest him for stealing. The poor swagman did not want to be caught alive and hanged, so he sprang into the billabong and drowned himself. From that day on, you could always hear his ghost haunting when you were passing the billabong.
When summarising the content of the song in their own words, the students could also substitute English words, definitions or explanations for the strine words (swagman, jumbuck, etc.).

Brett Whiteley – One of Australia's Avant-Garde Artists

Das Foto auf Seite 27 zeigt ein imposantes Werk des Avantgarde-Künstlers Brett Whiteley. Es symbolisiert das für Australien so typische Nebeneinander von Alt und Neu, Jung und Alt vor dem Hintergrund einer Stadt, die das Gleiche erkennen lässt: die einem alten englischen Architekturstil verpflichtete Marienkirche (*St Mary's Catholic Cathedral*) und daneben den hochmodernen Sydney Tower inmitten der City.
Der Text ist geeignet für stilles Lesen. Die Thematik lässt sich mit Recherchen in Lexika und im Internet schnell um weitere Künstler der australischen Moderne erweitern, wie z. B. Arthur Boyd, John Passmore, John Perceval, Sidney Nolan, Danila Vassilieff, Joy Hester oder Albert Tucker.

Solutions

Activities p. 27

1. **Describe Whiteley's work "Almost once". Try to interpret it.**
   At first, the students might just describe what they see in the entire picture (impressive monument of two big matches, a person looking at the monument, park with lawn and trees in the foreground, behind it a sportsground on the left side, in the background the city with skyscrapers, church and tower).
   After this they may try to interpret the monument itself. It shows two giant matches, one is new, the other one is used and is almost completely burnt down to the base. Obviously, these symbolise young and old, new and used, etc.

2. **Imagine you are visiting Sydney. Write an email to a German friend of yours in which you tell him or her about Brett Whiteley and what you think was especially fascinating about him.**
   Individual answers. Instead of an email, the students could write a letter. The teacher should direct the students' attention to the different conventions for emails and letters.

3. **Search the web for more information about the other artists mentioned in the text: Arthur Boyd and John Passmore.**
   After searching the web and finding out information about Aboriginal and non-Aboriginal artists, the students could decorate the classroom with illustrations and texts about these people.
   Some of the pictures of these artists can be found in the online arts encyclopaedia www.artcyclopedia.com/artists/boyd_jr_arthur.html.

Finnikin of the Rock

Melina Marchetta

Author and text

M. Marchetta ist in Deutschland bereits mit ihrem Erstlingsroman „Looking for Alibrandi" bekannt geworden (herausgegeben im Ernst Klett Verlag). Inzwischen werden ihre jugendgemäßen Romane in vielen Ländern gelesen und gehören zur Schullektüre im Englischunterricht.

"Her first novel *Looking for Alibrandi* swept the pool of literary awards for young adult fiction in 1993, winning the Children's Book Council of Australia (CBCA) Book of the Year Award (Older Readers). In 2000, it was released as a major Australian film, winning, among others, the Film Critics Circle of Australia Award. Melina Marchetta taught secondary school English and History for ten years, during which time she released her second novel, *Saving Francesca*, in 2003, followed by *On the Jellicoe Road* in 2006."

(From the back cover text of the book *Finnikin of the Rock*)

Im vorliegenden Text wird das 2008 in Australien erschienene Werk *Finnikin of the Rock* vorgestellt, das unter anderem bei Penguin Books erschienen ist. Darin geht es um die fiktive Figur des Finnikin, der in einer halbimaginären Welt von Phantomen und Göttern viele Abenteuer erlebt. Das Buch ist trotz seines etwas größeren Umfangs gut für den Unterricht geeignet.
Hier ein Zitat aus der Buchbesprechung bei Penguin Books:

"Finnikin of the Rock and his guardian, Sir Topher, have not been home to their beloved Lumatere for ten years. Not since the dark days when the royal family was murdered and the kingdom put under a terrible curse. But then Finnikin is summoned to meet Evanjalin, a young woman with an incredible claim: the heir to the throne of Lumatere, Prince Balthazar, is alive. Evanjalin is determined to return home and she is the only one who can lead them to the heir. As they journey together, Finnikin is affected by her arrogance ... and her hope. He begins to believe he will see his childhood friend, Prince Balthazar, again. And that their cursed people will be able to enter Lumatere and be reunited with those trapped inside. He even believes he will find his imprisoned father. But Evanjalin is not what she seems. And the truth will test not only Finnikin's faith in her ... but in himself."

Solutions

1. **Read the text. Then retell the beginning of the story in your own words. Concentrate on the situation, plot and characters of the story.** Activities p. 28
   Example:
   Finnikin sees someone in the distance and wonders if it might be a phantom. He has heard that this land at the end of the world has been forsaken by the gods. Suddenly, he catches sight of the cloister of the Goddess Lagrami at the top of a rock. In addition, Finnikin can see some pilgrims wandering across the country.
   One of them, the King's First Man, says in the Sarnak language that they had better hurry. He wants it to appear they have come from a neighbouring kingdom and thus has started to use this language here. The pilgrims are holy men who have come to the end of the earth to worship the Goddess.
   As they get closer, the ground under their feet begins to change into a sick clay-like substance making walking very hard. They are walking on a sea bed. By night the waters will return, so they have to hurry.
   Characters:
   Finnikin, Sir Topher, the pilgrims
   Situation:
   Finnikin and the pilgrims are walking across the waste land of Sendecane
   Plot: see above

2. **Guess how the story could go on. Discuss.**
   Individual answers. The teacher should accept any continuation, whether funny, fantastic or tragic. The main idea of this task is to give students the chance to show imagination and to practise creative writing.

3. **Write down the possible structure of the whole narrative on one page: introduction, main part, conclusion. Then compare your ideas.**
The following example has nothing to do with the real story of the book. It is given simply to show how the students, too, might be creative and develop a story of their own.
Example:
Introduction – see above
Main part – the pilgrims initially find a new home in their neighbouring kingdom but eventually get into trouble with the people there and end up having to fight them; Finnikin falls in love with a princess of the other country
Conclusion – the pilgrims triumph over their enemies but feel forced to leave this country; the love story thus ends tragically
The students can compare their ideas for the story in groups or as a whole class. If they want to, they might also write up more complete stories at home.

4. **Find out more about the author. Who is she? What does she write?**
Melina Marchetta (*1965) was born in Sydney to a family of Italian descent. For ten years, she worked as a teacher at St Mary's Cathedral College, where she taught English and History. Her first novel, *Looking for Alibrandi*, published in 1993, won the Children's Book Council of Australia "Book of the Year Award" as well as many other awards. The story was also released as a major Australian film in 2000 and won the AFI Award and the Independent Film Award for best screenplay. Her second novel *Saving Francesca* followed in 2003. *On the Jellicoe Road* and *Finnikin of the Rock* are her latest works. Her books have been published in more than fourteen countries and eleven languages. Today, Melina Marchetta is a full-time writer.

Australia

Baz Luhrmann

Die australische Filmproduktion ist seit der zweiten Hälfte des 20. Jahrhunderts, obwohl quantitativ begrenzt, international bekannt geworden. Filme wie „Crocodile Dundee", „Rabbit-Proof Fence" (in den deutschen Kinos erschienen unter dem Titel „The Long Walk Home") und „Australia" wurden weltweit gesehen („Australia" z. B. von bisher 23 Millionen Menschen; 2009).
Die wohl informativste Seite über die Kinematografie in Australien ist www.australia-movie.net. Aber auch Wikipedia bietet eine kurze chronologische Übersicht und Links zu Filmen, Produzenten und Schauspielern.

Solutions

Activities p. 29

1. **Describe the main characters starring in the film. To what extent do they reflect Australian history?**
Lady Sarah Ashley (acted by Nicole Kidman) is an English aristocratic woman who, in this film, represents the British settlers and immigrants to Australia.
Drover (Hugh Jackman) is a cattle drover, who stands for the white working or farming class in Outback Australia.
Nullah (Brandon Walters) is a half-caste Aboriginal boy who, together with his family and his grandfather, is part of the Indigenous population of Australia.

The characters and the plot reflect early British settlement in Australia, when the Aboriginal tribes were driven off their homelands so that white settlers and farmers could work and farm the land, which often belonged to wealthy British aristocrats.

2. **What is meant by the term "Stolen Generations"? Search the web to find out more about this issue.**
The term "Stolen Generations" refers to those Indigenous children who were forcibly taken away from their parents to be "educated" in white missions and government institutions. The removals began around 1869. In some areas, however, children were still being removed as late as the 1970s.
The extract from "Stolen" by Jane Harrison on page 57 is dedicated to this theme. A good website about the Stolen Generations is www.eniar.org/stolengenerations.html.

3. **Do you know any of the above-mentioned titles or perhaps another famous Australian film? Choose a film and tell your classmates about it.**
Individual answers. The students might know such films as "The Castle", "The Dish", "Ten Canoes", "Somersault", "Crocodile Dundee", "Rabbit-Proof Fence", "The Adventures of Priscilla, Queen of the Desert", "Shine", "Love and other Catastrophies", or the above-mentioned "Looking for Alibrandi". For more about Australian films in Germany, see www.australien-info.de/kino.html.

"Neighbours" – An Australian TV Soap

Ähnlich wie in den USA, Großbritannien oder Deutschland sind Fernsehsoaps auch in Australien sehr beliebt. Ältere Soaps sind „The Young Doctors“, „The Sullivans“ oder „Sons and Daughters“, immer noch auf dem Bildschirm ist 2009 die Serie „Neighbours“, die bereits 1985 gestartet wurde, und „Home and Away“, die 1988 anfing. Der Text auf Seite 30 beschreibt ein werbewirksames Event der Produzenten von „Neighbours“, nämlich die *Neighbours Night*.
Dieses Thema wird jene Schüler besonders ansprechen, die deutsche Seifenopern wie „Gute Zeiten, schlechte Zeiten“ gern sehen, und sie anregen, diese mit dem australischen Produkt zu vergleichen.

Solutions

Activities p. 31

1. **What event do "Neighbours" fans celebrate once a week in Australia? Describe what goes on at these events.**
Once a week, "Neighbours" fans celebrate Neighbours Night. This special event, which is usually held at a venue in Melbourne, but also sometimes in Sydney, includes a trivia quiz, live music and the chance for fans to meet actors from the soap. The event is also sometimes used for charity purposes. Thus, for example, a concert given by a range of famous Australian and international bands as part of the Neighbours Night on 16 February, 2009, along with an auction of "Neighbours" memorabilia raised A$ 31,105.50, which was donated to the Red Cross in order to support the victims of the disastrous bushfires in that month.

2. **Who usually profits from these events? Analyse the reasons why they are organised. Think about this question carefully, then discuss your answers.**
The biggest part of the profit, of course, goes to the owners of the tourism companies that organize the events, as well as the TV production company – Fremantle

Media – and the TEN network and the actors who take part in it. A minor part goes to charity on special occasions.
In analysing the reasons why *Neighbours Nights* and other commercial activities are organized, the students should work out that the production company and the TV network, of course, want to entertain the people, but above all, they want to get more and more people to watch this soap opera and thus make a huge profit.

3. **Do you know of similar events or other advertising strategies in Germany? If so, tell your classmates about them.**
Individual answers.

4. **"GZSZ" is not on the tube yet in Australia. Imagine you are publicity consultants who have been given the task to make this series popular Down Under. In groups of four to five, think up potential strategies. Finally, introduce your ideas to the class and decide which strategies would probably be most effective.**
The students should form groups of four or five to develop their strategies. In working out their ideas, the students will be forced to express in English what they know about German soaps or to translate some texts into English, thus mediating between the two cultures. After fifteen minutes of work, the students can present their ideas in any way they choose.

5. **Why not celebrate Australia Day (on 26 January) by having an Australia Party in your class? There is not much you need to do.**
The teacher, together with the class, can decide whether they want to have such a party. If so, the party will be a good chance to repeat and practise what the students have learned so far.
If the class does decide to have an Australia Party, the teacher might want to discuss the following issues with the students:
– How can we best create an Australian atmosphere? For example, we could play Aboriginal music, or sing popular songs: http://home.iprimus.com.au/gunnado/songs.html.
– We could also decorate the room, for example, with a map of Australia, some typical souvenirs such as a didgeridoo or another indigenous musical instrument, a toy kangaroo, some postcards, etc. The school or community library is sure to have books about Australia. Alternatively, we could try contacting the Australian embassy in Berlin or asking local travel agencies for brochures and other relevant material.
– Are there any particular kinds of refreshments or food we could buy in the supermarket? We could try to find, for example, Australian apples, macadamia nuts, or even New Zealand kiwi fruit or honey, thus making it a general Down Under Party, including both Australia and New Zealand.

Multicultural Australia

Australien ist über seine gesamte Entwicklung in der Neuzeit (seit seiner Erstbesiedlung durch Europäer 1788) ein Land der Immigranten. In diesem Kapitel erhalten die Schüler Informationen über den zahlenmäßigen Anteil von Einwanderern der ersten, zweiten und weiteren Generationen an der Gesamtbevölkerung des Landes und lernen Australier und ihre Lebensgeschichte, aber auch die im Vielvölkerstaat immer wieder auftretenden Probleme kennen.
Detaillierte Angaben über die Immigrationspolitik sowie Statistiken dazu sind unter anderem zu finden auf der Webpräsenz des Statistischen Amts Australiens (*Australian Bureau of Statistics*): www.ausstats.abs.gov.au/ausstats/subscriber.nsf/LookupAttach/2070.0Publication29.01.0910/$File/20700_Cultural_overview.pdf.

What Place Multiculturalism?

Peter Jensen

In diesem Text äußert sich ein prominenter Bürger Australiens, Dr. Peter Jensen, Erzbischof von Sydney, zum Wesen und den Problemen der Multikultur in seinem Land. Seine Ausführungen können den Schülern als Anregung dienen, auch über die multikulturelle Bevölkerung in Deutschland nachzudenken und die damit verbundenen Vorteile und Probleme zu diskutieren.

Far and Near

Ouyang Yu

Das kurze Gedicht „Far and Near" auf Seite 33 bedarf keiner umfangreichen Interpretation, es spricht für sich selbst. Mit seiner eindeutigen Aussage („I am as far from any Australians as China is from Australia.") kann es in die Diskussion zu diesem Thema einbezogen werden.
Der Autor des Gedichts Ouyang Yu wurde in China geboren, hat dort den Bachelor und Master in Englischer und Amerikanischer Literatur abgelegt und wanderte 1991 nach Australien ein. Eine ausführlichere Biografie enthält die Webseite www.ouyangyu.com.au.

I never knew this about Australia

Die hier vorgelegten Daten über die Immigration in Australien werden durch passende Fotografien auf den Seiten dieses Kapitels illustriert. Die Ausführungen unter dem letzten Aufzählungspunkt untermauern das im Text von Peter Jensen Gesagte über den Einfluss verschiedener Religionen auf die australische Gesellschaft.
Zum Thema „Multikultur" sind viele Seiten im Internet zu finden. Zwei besonders interessante sind: www.multiculturalaustralia.edu.au/ und www.multiculturalaustralia.edu.au/history/.

Solutions

Activities p. 34

1. **Sum up how Peter Jensen sees multiculturalism in Australia.**
   Peter Jensen thinks that, in Australia, the word "multiculturalism" is no longer useful, because it seems to imply that Australia does not have any culture at all, neither British culture (as it still may have had 50 years ago), nor basic Australian culture. Without its own cultural basis, the Australian society will not be able to face future challenges. Jensen realizes that more and more immigrants from different countries of the world are dominating the streets of Australia. He is afraid that his church, the Anglican Church (the old Church of England), will not survive unless it learns to cater to other nationalities rather than just the British people, in particular to Asian people.
   On the other hand, he hopes that all of these people will speak English and to be more precise: Australian English. Only this common language will enable people to communicate with each other. Australian English has the potential to unite the people coming to Australia from all parts of the world and to enrich Australian society.

2. **Today, people of all faiths are welcome in Australia. Which future for religious life does Jensen foresee for his country? What do you learn from the text about multiculturalism in Australia? Discuss.**
   The first part of the task involves a summary, which may be given orally or in written form, whereas the second part asks the students to discuss this topic. The best way to do this could be a debate, ideally led by one of the students.

3. **Explain what your idea of ethnical multiculturalism is.**
   Individual answers.

4. **Imagine you are asked to write an article on immigration to Germany for your partner school. Collect information: How many immigrants are there in Germany? When did they come? Where do they come from? What problems do they have? etc.**
   This is a challenging task which should be given to the students as homework. The students will be able to find the data needed for their writing in various encyclopaedias or on the Internet, for example, on the websites: www.bamf.de/, www.destatis.de or www.magazine-deutschland.de/en/artikel-en/article/article/analyse-zuwanderung-und-integration-in-deutschland.html. As most of the sources are in German, the students will have to translate or mediate them.

Neighbours

Tim Winton

Im Schülerbuch (Seiten 35–38) ist die ungekürzte Geschichte des populären australischen Autors Tim Winton (*1960) abgedruckt. Sie ist der von Mary Lord herausgegebenen Sammlung *Best Australian Short Stories* (Penguin Books) entnommen, die noch weitere das australische Leben schildernde Kurzgeschichten enthält, die für die Lektüre im Englischunterricht der Oberstufe sehr gut geeignet sind.
Tim Winton ist bei seinen Lesern sehr beliebt. Unter anderem sind von ihm *Dirt Music*, *Riders* und *Land's Edge* erschienen. In der Kurzgeschichte „Neighbours" werden die Probleme einer neu zugezogenen Einwandererfamilie in einem Stadtviertel an der Ostküste Australiens beschrieben. Die Story eignet sich ausgezeichnet für das häusliche Lesen und die anschließende Besprechung im Unterricht.

Weitere für die Oberstufe empfehlenswerte *short stories* sind zum Beispiel die folgenden.

- **Price Warung** (William Astley): How Muster-Master Stoneman Earned His Breakfast (1892) – Eine erschreckende Geschichte aus der Zeit, als Australien noch eine Sträflingskolonie war.
- **Henry Lawson**: The Drover's Wife (1892) – Henry Lawson ist Australiens bekanntester Schriftsteller bis Mitte des 20. Jahrhunderts. Er wurde als der erste *truly Australian writer* und *the voice of the bush* bezeichnet. Seine Kurzgeschichte „The Drover's Wife" ist die australische Erzählung schlechthin. Sie singt das Hohelied auf eine australische Frau im Überlebenskampf mit der Natur (einer Schlange im Haus).
- **Thea Astley**: Heart Is Where the Home Is (1989) – Thea Astley, ehemals Schul- und Hochschullehrerin in Queensland, gehörte in den 70er-/80er-Jahren zu jenen, die die Welle des *women's writing* in Australien auslösten und damit sehr bekannt wurden. Die Geschichte „Heart Is Where the Home Is" erzählt eine anrührende Begebenheit aus der Zeit der *Stolen Generations* (Australien in den 20ern bis hinein in die 60er-Jahre des 20. Jahrhunderts): *Police officers* kommen in eine Siedlung der Aborigines, nehmen den Familien mit Gewalt die Kinder weg, um sie unter Weißen aufziehen zu lassen, und eine junge Mutter flieht mit ihrem Kind in den Busch ...

Auf der Bildseite von **Worksheet 2** werden einige der genannten und weitere bedeutende australische Schriftsteller vorgestellt, für die runde Gedenkplatten in den Fußboden rings um den *Circular Quay* von Sydney eingelassen sind. Die Bilder können zum Betrachten mit den Schülern auf eine Folie kopiert werden. In Vorbereitung dieses Unterrichtsschritts werden den Schülern einige Stunden vorher Aufträge dazu erteilt, z. B. die Biografien der Autoren vorzubereiten und ausgewählte Werke dieser Schriftsteller vorzustellen.

Solutions

Activities p. 38

1. **Determine what type of text this is. Give reasons and examples to explain why you think so.**
   The text is a short story. Short stories are characterized by a small number of characters (here: the young couple and their neighbours) and a limited setting (in this story, everything happens in and around the couple's house). Short stories are also, as the name suggests, typically very short, generally comprising just a few pages.

2. **Read the text twice. Afterwards, give an oral or written summary of the story in about 100 words.**
   Summary:
   A young couple moves into a new house in a district full of European immigrants. At first, they feel annoyed by their neighbours' curious looks and loud, seemingly unfriendly behaviour. However, when the neighbours notice that the young woman is pregnant, they become very friendly and start to help the couple in many ways. By late summer, a woman next door has knitted the baby a suit, and a Polish neighbour brings them wood for their fire. In winter, after the woman has given birth to a boy, the heartfelt compassion and support of their neighbours makes the young family feel very comfortable in their new home. (107 words)

3. Make a grid to show visually how the single characters and their behaviour develop. Comment on this development.

Example:

Character	Behaviour
young man	At the beginning, he feels uncomfortable and is quite shocked, as is his wife. While working on his doctor's thesis, he senses the disapproval of their neighbours at his staying at home (and writing) while his wife goes out to work. In disgust, he watches the little boy next door urinating in the street and even spraying his car. It makes him nervous as he feels he is being watched by their neighbours, who seem to be loud and unfriendly. Step by step, he begins to feel more comfortable when he and his wife start coming into contact with their neighbours and helping each other. Even further down the track, when he sees the friendly reactions of the neighbours to his wife and her baby, he feels completely settled in and at home.
young woman	She is not at home as often as her husband, and at the beginning of the story, seems not to have a real relationship to their neighbours. At first, she and her husband are shocked when they hear or see the neighbours talking loudly, spitting on the street or doing their washing, as this makes the newcomers feel quite uncomfortable. After some months, however, she dares to establish first contacts, for example, by stroking a little boy's shaven head. Later, she smiles back to their neighbours when they give and receive little gifts from the garden. When she gets pregnant, the young woman even begins to feel grateful when the neighbours start to care for her and her baby.
Macedonian family	The Macedonian family at first seems to be very rough and unfriendly because they are always talking very loudly and disapprove of the young couple's rising late in the morning. However, later they turn out to be very helpful and friendly. They show the young couple how to slaughter, pluck and dress hens. In the evenings, they sit together talking and telling each other stories. They wish the young woman and her baby all the best.
Polish widower	At first, the Polish widower gets on the young couple's nerves, because he is hammering all day and seems to work without rhyme or reason. However, one day he helps the newcomers to build a hen house; later he brings the young couple woodscraps for the fire and also turns out to be very friendly and helpful.
other people	The street is home to a multicultural neighbourhood. At the beginning, the neighbours do not know the newcomers. However, bit by bit, they become more familiar with them. When they learn that the young woman is pregnant, they become friendlier and friendlier. Some of them offer help and advice, others give little presents to the couple or show in other ways that they care about the baby. For example, some Italian women offer names for the baby, the Greek women feel the woman's belly and give her some good advice, and the woman next door knits a baby suit. Thus, in the end, all of the people have accepted the newcomers as good neighbours.

4. Work in two groups. One group writes a script based on this story. The other group produces a radio play. Alternatively, the whole class might act out the story as a role-play.

Individual answers expected. The writing group might think up a radio play that is quite different from the plot given in the short story. Regardless of whether the class produces a radio novel or a role play, acting out the story is bound to be great fun for them in any case.

City Welcomes New Citizens

Ein authentischer Bericht über die Empfangszeremonie für Neubürger und eine Statistiktabelle über die Einwandererzahlen aus den verschiedenen Ländern informieren die Schüler hier über die heutige Zusammensetzung der australischen Nation. Während der Lesetext geeignet ist für die Verständniskontrolle (Anforderungsbereich 1), verlangt bzw. wiederholt die Statistik den sicheren Umgang mit dem verstehenden Lesen und Interpretieren von Daten. Beides kann auch über die in den *Activities* aufgeführten Aufgaben hinaus geübt werden.

Solutions

Activities p. 39

1. **Where did these 'new citizens' come from? What were their reasons for emigrating?**
   In the report written by E. Himmelreich, the ten new Australian citizens came from Vietnam, the UK, Sudan and India.
   One of them (Trung Tran from Vietnam) said that he had followed his sister and her family to Australia because he was seeking a more challenging life and wanted to get an IT job here.
   Phil Whipple from India, who had spent many years in the United States, decided to become a citizen of Australia because he just loved the country.
   There are no facts given about the reasons why the other people came to Australia. They, too, probably had the wish to improve their situation, to earn more money, to join their family, or just to enjoy life in Australia.

2. **Interpret the table. What migration trends does it reveal?**
   The table "Generations in Australia – 2006" can be interpreted from many different points of view. It is interesting, however, to note and discuss, for example, the following facts:
   – more than seven million people describe themselves as Australian-born,
   – the largest number of immigrants come from England, Ireland and Scotland,
   – almost one million people are of German descent,
   – compared to the 3rd-plus generation Australians (whose ancestors mainly came from Ireland – 80.1 %, Scotland – 77.3 %, and Germany – 74.1 %), 1st generation Australians nowadays come, above all, from India (77.6 %).

3. **Find out who L. Leichhardt, H. Heysen and W. Blass were and which part they played in Australian history and society. Write a brief sketch of their lives and display it in your classrom.**
   These three men are famous German-Australians, and are extremely well-known, not only for their achievements in Australia, but also for the heritage they brought them as immigrants to Australia and as ethnic Germans.
   Friedrich Wilhelm Ludwig Leichhardt (1813 – 1848?): Leichhardt studied Philosophy, Languages and Natural Sciences at the Universities of Berlin and Göttingen. In 1837, he moved to England, where he continued his education in natural sciences at various places, including the British Museum in London. He also studied at the Jardin des Plantes in Paris and undertook field studies in several European countries including Italy and Switzerland. In 1842, Leichhardt moved to Sydney, where he led three major expeditions across Australia, through the Outback. On his last expedition, he disappeared without a trace and thus, nobody knows exactly when and where he died.

Leichhardt was certainly accepted as an adoptive local by the Australians since his interest in Australia was by no means just a passing phase in the country's history.

Sir Wilhelm Ernst Hans Franz Heysen (1877–1968) was a German-Australian artist who was particularly well-known for his watercolour paintings of the Australian bush. He migrated to Adelaide in South Australia with his family in 1884 at the age of 7, and even as a young boy, showed an early interest in art. At the age of 14, he left school to work for a hardware merchant, later studying Art at night school and in any other spare time he had. By 1912, Heysen had earned enough from his art to purchase a property called "The Cedars" near Hahndorf in the Adelaide Hills, which remained his home until he died in 1968 aged 90. To this day, Hans Heysen is still one of the most popular painters in Australia. His name graces everything from walking trails to freeway tunnels.

Wolf Blass (*1934) is the most readily recognized name of any individual Barossa Valley wine-maker. Born in East Germany, Blass arrived in Australia in 1961, and soon became Australia's first consultant winemaker before setting up his own winery in the late sixties. It is in this famous wine-making valley that German culture has really made its mark on Australian cultural life.

NB: The website of the Immigration Museum of Melbourne offers a lot of interesting articles about immigration and immigrants, and also biographies of German immigrants to Australia. See also:
– www.adb.online.anu.edu.au
– www.wolfblass.com.au

Australia and Me – Interview with Stephen O'Grady

Die meisten Nationalitätengruppen, die in Australien eingewandert sind, haben ihre eigenen Medien. In ihnen wird unter anderem darüber berichtet, wie es den Landsleuten in Australien ergeht. Meistens sind derartige Berichte positiv, Probleme werden allerdings auch nicht verschwiegen. In diesem Text aus der Zeitung „Irish Echo" wird der irische Journalist Stephen O'Grady in einem Interview vorgestellt.
Bei der Behandlung dieses Textes kann die Lehrkraft auf die Besonderheiten der Textsorte Interview eingehen: kurze prägnante, persönliche Fragen, sehr persönliche Antworten in der Ich-Form, Gebrauch der Zeitform des Präsens.

Solutions

Activities p. 40

1. **Is Stephen happy and satisfied that he has come to Australia? Give reasons.**
   In the interview, Stephen says that he works as a journalist for a daily regional paper (the "Fraser Coast Chronicle"), which is a different challenge for him. Although he complains that he does not have much time for fun, he was involved in a drama group, playing the Reverend John Hale in Arthur Miller's "The Crucible", which was in fact lots of fun. He has also starred in a short film, and at the weekend, he typically enjoys drinking a few beers and watching National Rugby League. All of this shows that Stephen does indeed seem to be happy and satisfied in Australia.

2. **Do you know anyone who came to Germany as a first generation immigrant? Try asking them the questions of this interview. You may also add more questions. Write the answers down.**
   The students may think up a list of questions of their own. They might, however, also use the questionnaire given on **Worksheet 3**.

We Are Australians – Letters from Immigrants (I and II)

Auf den Seiten 41 und 42 des Schülerbuchs werden den Lesern zwei authentische Briefe von Einwanderern aus Deutschland und Österreich vorgelegt, die die Betreffenden dankenswerterweise eigens für diesen Zweck geschrieben haben. In ihnen werden die Gründe und Umstände der Auswanderung beschrieben. Aus ihrem Inhalt geht aber auch hervor, welche Gefühle die Australier ihrer neuen und der alten Heimat gegenüber hegen. Ein Beispiel für die Traditionspflege bieten die Fotos auf den Seiten 41 unten und 42 oben, auf denen zu sehen ist, wie der *German Club* zu einer Festlichkeit zusammenkommt.
Die Briefe können den Schülern als Anregung dienen, Bürger zu interviewen, die nach Deutschland eingewandert sind, und deren Lebensgeschichte zu erfahren. Dies kann zu mehr gegenseitigem Verständnis und interkultureller Akzeptanz führen.
Ähnliche Lebensberichte, allerdings von Immigranten aus Asien, sind auch zu finden auf der Webseite www.migrationheritage.nsw.gov.au („Stories from South Asia to Sydney").

Solutions

Activities p. 42

1. **How do Anni and Bruno feel about their Australian citizenship?**
Both Anni und Bruno feel proud and happy to be Australians. However, they have not forgotten their former homeland and do a lot to keep up their Austrian/German traditions and culture.

2. **Ask the ten questions the two are seemingly answering in their letters.**
It seems, the two people answer the following questions:
(1) Where do you come from?
(2) Why did you come to Australia?
(3) What were your first impressions of the new country?
(4) Did you have any difficulties with the English language?
(5) Did you experience any highlights?
(6) Where and how do you live today?
(7) Do you preserve the culture of your ancestors? How?
(8) Do you sometimes still speak German?
(9) What are your feelings about Australia?
(10) Are you proud to be Australian?

3. **To what extent do their life stories correspond with the data given in the table "Generations in Australia" on page 39?**
The life stories told in these two letters correspond with the data given in the table "Generations in Australia" to the extent that these two people belong to the large number of Germans of the 3rd-plus generation who came to Australia in round about the middle of the 20th century.

4. **Do you know any people who came to Germany to live and work? If not, search for famous people who have chosen Germany as their new home. Present what you have learned about them to the class.**
The teacher might form groups of students or give special tasks to some of them in order to limit the number of presentations about immigrants to Germany. The students are allowed to determine the form of presentation. They could, for example, give five-minute talks or a short PowerPoint presentation.

Citizenship Testing

Seit 2007 müssen die Kandidaten für eine Einbürgerung in Australien einen Citizenship Test ablegen. Wenn sie ihn bestehen, dann wird ihnen ein *Certificate of Australian Citizenship* ausgehändigt. Einzelheiten dazu erfahren die Schüler aus dem Text „Citizenship testing".
Die Abbildung des Zertifikats im **Worksheet 4** ist anonymisiert worden, enthält aber genügend Details, die die Schüler daraus entnehmen und erörtern können. Dazu fertigt die Lehrkraft eine Folienkopie an.
Dieser Lesetext ist eine ausgezeichnete Grundlage für die weitere Beschäftigung mit den Bedingungen für die Einreise und Einwanderung nach Australien, aber auch für die Diskussion der Einreisebestimmungen in Deutschland.
Nähere Ausführungen über die Bedingungen für eine Einbürgerung in Australien enthalten zum Beispiel die Webseiten www.immi.gov.au und www.frankston.vic.gov.au. Sie sind auch dafür geeignet, von einigen Schülern im Unterricht vorgestellt zu werden. Andere Schüler könnten einen Vergleich mit den Einbürgerungsbestimmungen in Deutschland anstellen (z. B. mithilfe der Links www.zuwanderung.de oder – über den Einbürgerungstest – www.fluechtlingsrat-nrw.de/2862/) und dabei mediatorisch tätig werden.

Solutions

Activities p. 43

1. **Skim all texts of this chapter (pp. 32 to 43) to find out which values are held in high esteem in multicultural Australia.**
   The book "Becoming an Australian Citizen" edited by the Government of Australia lists the following values as being especially important:
   – respect for the equal worth, dignity and freedom of the individual,
   – freedom of speech,
   – freedom of religion and secular government,
   – freedom of association,
   – support for parliamentary democracy and the rule of law,
   – equality of men and women,
   – equality of opportunity,
   – peacefulness, tolerance, mutual respect and compassion for those in need.
   These are, of course, the officially-proclaimed values. In addition, the Australians themselves hold the following personal and official values in high esteem, some more than others depending on their original nationality. In general, they are proud of Australia and its history, proud to serve their adopted country, as well as being proud of the country they have originally come from, proud of both the Western and happy to be part of the Aboriginal culture of Australia, and the indigenous relaxed, open and friendly culture that Australians are famous for.

2. **What feelings do immigrants have when they look back at their coming Down Under and staying there? Discuss.**
   According to what Anni Radle and Bruno Schwaerzler have written in their letters, most of the new Australians look back at their native country with positive feelings and some of them may even long for the homeland of their parents and grandparents. The teacher may discuss with the class what feelings the students could imagine having if they were to leave their homes in Germany and move to another country.

3. **This is Australia's Citizenship Pledge:**
   "From this time forward, under God, I pledge my loyalty to Australia and its People, whose democratic beliefs I share, whose rights and liberties I respect, and whose laws I will uphold and obey."
   (A person may choose to make the Pledge with or without the words 'under God'.) Interpret these words. What would keeping this pledge mean to a new citizen of Australia?
   A first point to note is that the Pledge can be chosen to be made with or without the words "under God". This shows that the government is in fact keeping its pledge to respect the above-mentioned human right to freedom of religion. In this short statement, Australia declares itself to be a democratic country whose beliefs, rights and liberties must be respected and whose laws must be upheld and obeyed.
   For every new citizen of Australia, keeping this pledge means not only just knowing the values listed above, but also respecting them.

4. **Is there a citizenship test for immigrants who want to become a citizen of Germany? Do new citizens of our country have to take a citizenship pledge, too? Should they have to? Hold a class debate on this topic. Discuss the pros and cons.**
   There is indeed now a citizenship test for immigrants to Germany (Einbürgerungstest). It was introduced in 2008 and contains 33 questions, of which at least 17 must be answered correctly to pass the test.
   In the discussion, the students should consider the pros and cons of such a test and whether they are for or against the introduction of a similar Pledge to that in Australia and many other countries. See the "Gesetzentwurf des Bundesrates" for a German Citizenship Pledge: www.umwelt-online.de/cgi-bin/parser/Drucksachen/drucknews.cgi?texte=0067_2D05B.

Worksheet 2

Famous Australian Writers

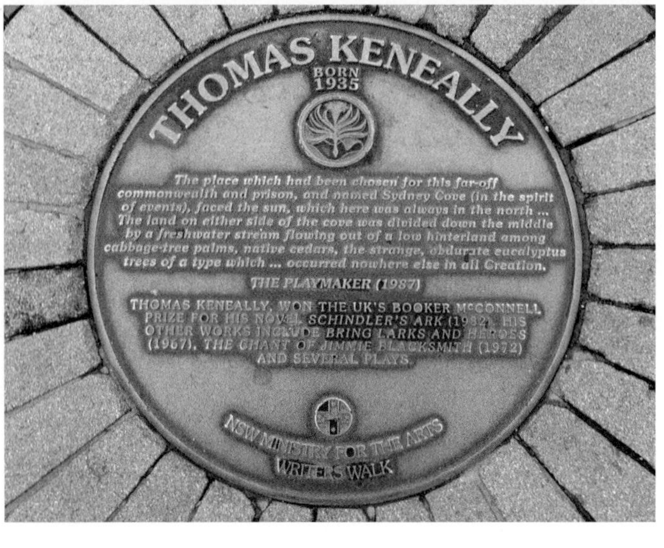

Fotos: © Rainer H. Berthelmann

Worksheet 3

Interview

- What is your background and why did you come to Germany?

- Describe what you do here.

- Did you have difficulties with the German language when you first arrived?

- Did you have any difficulties in everyday life when you first arrived?

- Do you like Germany? What do you do for fun?

- How do you preserve the culture of your ancestors? Do you sometimes visit your relatives in your home country?

- How has your life changed since you came to Germany?

- ______________________________

- ______________________________

Worksheet 4

Certificate of Australian Citizenship

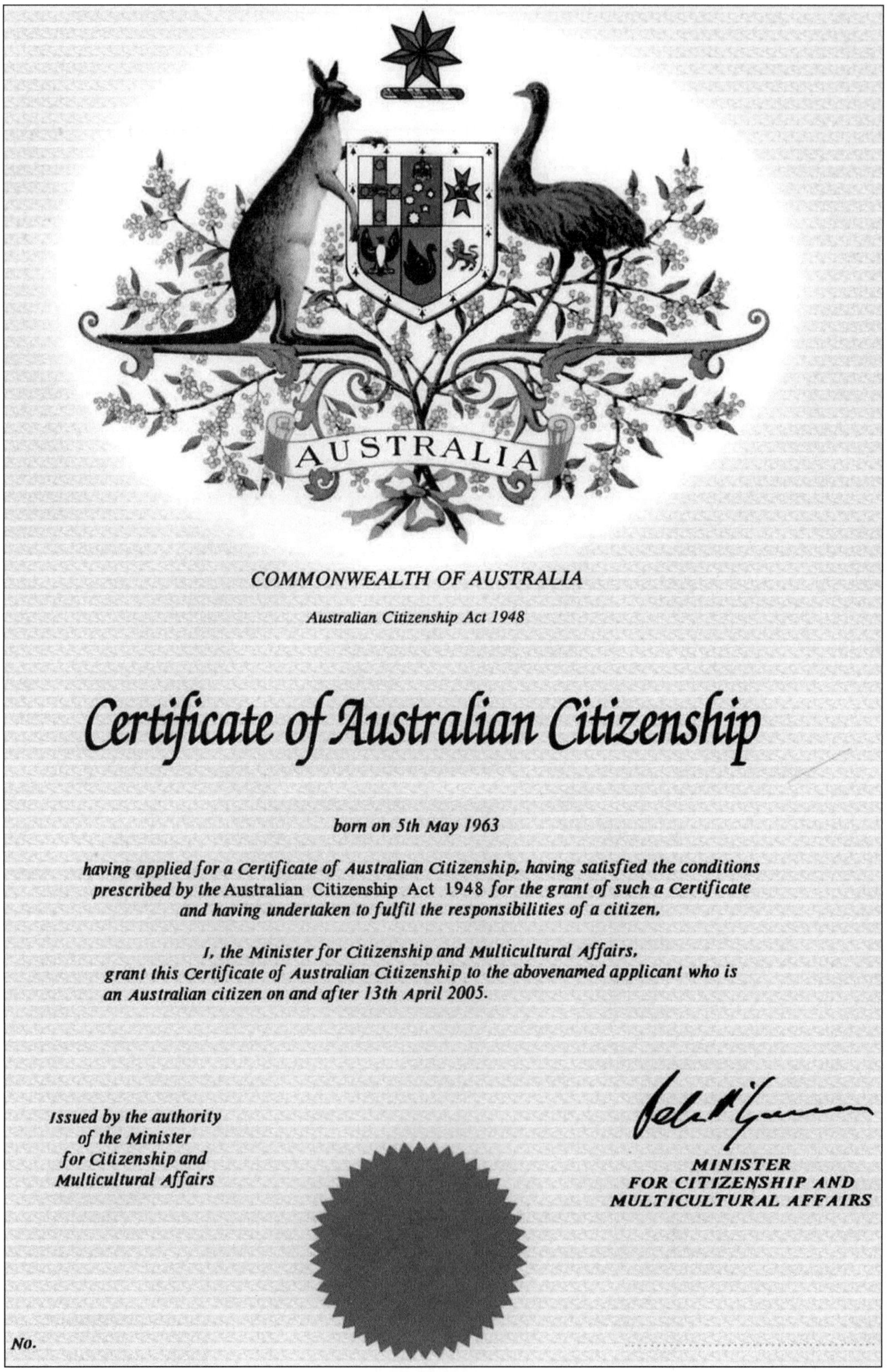

AUSTRALIA

COMMONWEALTH OF AUSTRALIA

Australian Citizenship Act 1948

Certificate of Australian Citizenship

born on 5th May 1963

having applied for a Certificate of Australian Citizenship, having satisfied the conditions prescribed by the Australian Citizenship Act 1948 *for the grant of such a Certificate and having undertaken to fulfil the responsibilities of a citizen,*

I, the Minister for Citizenship and Multicultural Affairs, grant this Certificate of Australian Citizenship to the abovenamed applicant who is an Australian citizen on and after 13th April 2005.

Issued by the authority of the Minister for Citizenship and Multicultural Affairs

MINISTER FOR CITIZENSHIP AND MULTICULTURAL AFFAIRS

No.

Outback but not Back of Bourke

Die Landschaft und das Leben im Herzen Australiens (in the *Red Centre*) unterscheiden sich von denen entlang der Küste erheblich. Zwei besonders ins Auge fallende Unterschiede sind die *School of the Air* und der *Royal Flying Doctor Service*.
Die Texte über diese beiden australischen Einrichtungen tangieren die Schüler sicherlich auf besondere Weise. Vor allem der authentische Brief der Schülerin einer 1500 km von der *cattle station* ihrer Eltern entfernten *boarding school* über ihre Zeit als Teilnehmerin an der *School of the Air* wird Veranlassung geben zum Nachdenken und zu weiteren Nachfragen. Aber auch die technisch komplizierte Bewerkstelligung der medizinischen Versorgung von Einwohnern und Touristen im Outback wird das Interesse der Schüler finden und sie vielleicht motivieren, mehr darüber erfahren zu wollen.

School of the Air

Im Mittelpunkt dieses Beitrags steht der kindlich geschriebene Brief von Shannon, in dem sie von der Zeit erzählt, als sie bis zur 7. Klasse die *Alice Springs School of the Air* besuchte.
Die vier Bilder auf der Seite 44 verschaffen eine plastische Vorstellung von der Landschaft und dem Leben im Outback:
Hinter Glas können Besucher der *School of the Air* den zentralen „Unterrichtsraum" sehen, in dem die Lehrkräfte mithilfe modernster Technik mit den zum Teil sehr weit entfernt wohnenden Schülern in Verbindung stehen. Zur Zeit dieser Aufnahme (2008) hatte die *School of the Air* in Alice Springs 114 Schüler.
Das Bild rechts daneben deutet die Wüstenlandschaft im Outback an. Zu sehen ist der kreisförmige Wuchs des Spinifexgrases, der durch die zirkulare Ausbreitung der Wurzeln dieser Pflanze zustande kommt.
Die beiden unteren Bilder zeigen den Wohnsitz (*homestead*) von Shannons Eltern auf der *cattle station* und den Computerarbeitsplatz des Mädchens. Shannons Familie stammt in zweiter Generation von irischen Einwanderern ab. Von ehemals 8000 Stück Vieh, die die Familie auf dem 40 000 km² großen Grundstück einst halten konnte, können heute aufgrund der anhaltenden Dürre der letzten Jahre nur noch 4000 ernährt werden.
Das beeindruckende Panoramabild auf der Seite 46 zeigt, wie unterschiedlich die Witterungsverhältnisse auch im Outback sein können: nach 40–50 Grad Hitze überrascht die Stadt urplötzlich ein gewaltiger Hurrikan, der Zerstörung und Verwüstung, aber auch das dringlich erwartete Wasser mit sich bringt.

I never knew this about Australia

Die dichten Informationen über die *School of Air*, die sich auf Seite 46 finden, sind abgefasst in der Form von *frequently asked questions*. Nachdem sie gelesen und erörtert wurden (beispielsweise könnte die Lehrkraft auf das internationale *Distance Learning* näher eingehen), ist es denkbar, dass die Schüler weitere *FAQs* formulieren und beantworten. Aus all diesem Wissen und mithilfe der Ergebnisse von Internetrecherchen kann zusätzlich zum *leaflet* oder an seiner Stelle eine Klassenraumpräsentation angefertigt werden.

Solutions

Activities p. 46

1. **Write an information leaflet for German-speaking tourists comprising the most important facts about the Alice Springs School of the Air.**
   In the leaflet, the students should give short information about what the 'School of the Air' is, and how it works. Furthermore, the text should contain some facts that the students consider to be important for tourists to read.
   This is intended as a mediating task as the students have to put into German what they have learned about the SOA. Alternatively, however, the teacher might decide to ask the class to produce a similar leaflet in English.

2. **Write a personal letter in which you ask Shannon more questions about the ASSOA, and tell her about a regular German school.**
   Individual answers, but the students should keep to the form of a letter. This means they should address their letter to a certain person, write in a personal style and conclude the letter appropriately.

Royal Flying Doctor Service

Der hier abgedruckte Text ist dem originalen *Information Leaflet* des *Royal Flying Doctor Service* entnommen. Er ist in unterschiedlichen Versionen auch im Internet zu finden. Zumindest können diese Texte für weitere Recherchen benutzt werden.
Der Sachtext ist relativ schwer zu lesen, vor allem weil er verschiedene technische Termini und Wendungen enthält. Er bietet sich deshalb zum Lesen mit dem einsprachigen oder sogar zweisprachigen Wörterbuch an. Da in den deutschen Bundesländern nach und nach wieder zweisprachige Wörterbücher in den Abiturprüfungen zugelassen werden, stellt dies eine gute Vorübung dar.
Die auf Seite 48 abgebildete Tabelle „Annual Statistics on the RFDS Australia 2008" gibt die originale Statistik verkürzt wieder, ist aber darum nicht weniger imposant. Da es den Schülern erfahrungsgemäß nicht leicht fällt, statistisches Material zu lesen und zu interpretieren, dies aber in den Bildungsstandards für die Sprache Englisch gefordert wird, kann die Lehrkraft dies hier als gesonderten Arbeitsschritt einfügen.
Die Fotografien unter der Tabelle von Seite 48 zeigen die Innenausstattung eines Flugzeugs, das eigens für das RFDS-Museum in Alice Springs angefertigt wurde. Die Dispatcherin im Bild links geht ihrer täglichen Arbeit nach, nämlich die eingehenden Hilferufe und Anforderungen zu registrieren, an das Ärzteteam weiterzuleiten und die Bereitschaft des Flugdienstes zu sichern.

Solutions

Activities p. 49

1. **Scan the text and the table to find out the answers to these questions:**
   a) **When did the RFDS start?**
   The world's first air ambulance, at that time known as the Aerial Medical Service, was officially started in 1928.
   b) **What area does the RFDS cover?**
   Today, RFDS covers an area of more than 7,150,000 km^2.
   c) **Who was its founder?**
   The founder of the Royal Flying Doctor Service was John Flynn (1880–1951), who not only started the Service, but also succeeded in organizing and improving the means of air transport, radio communication and medical aid.

d) **What technical equipment was used then, and what is used now?**
When the RFDS first started, there was no radio communication at all. However, soon after, Alfred Traeger developed a two-way radio set suitable for use on cattle or sheep stations. It was not until the 1970s that the Service finally underwent a major re-equipment programme and introduced the single sideband mode of transmission. Since the 1990s, the use of high frequency radio communication has dropped steadily, being increasingly substituted by standard and satellite telephones. Despite this, there is still the need to use the HF network, because some small communities, Aboriginal outstations, mobile phone users and tourists cannot connect to the standard telephone line when in the Outback far away from bigger settlements.

e) **How many people did the RFDS attend to in 2008?**
In 2008, a total of 105,800 people were attended to by the RFDS and received various kinds of help from the flying doctors.

f) **What did they have to pay for the service?**
The bulk of the medical help is free of charge to those people who live, work and travel in Australia's Outback.

g) **Comment on the importance of the RFDS.**
Individual answers. The students should, however, emphasize that, without the work of the RFDS, it would be impossible to make emergency flights in cases of serious illness or accidents. Any patient across the 80 % of Australia covered by the RFDS can be reached by the doctors within two hours.

2. **Discuss which effects on mankind great discoveries or inventions can have. Give examples from international or German history.**
Individual answers. The students could, for example, discuss the effects of the discoveries and inventions of Georg Cantor, Benjamin Franklin, Konrad Röntgen, Marie Curie, or Albert Einstein to name just a few.

3. **It was John Flynn's belief that "If you start an idea, nothing can stop it." This resulted in the creation of the Flying Doctor Service. What about you? Do you have any good ideas concerning, for example, your life, family, friends, or your school, town or society as a whole?**
Writing an essay on this topic could also be carried out as a class test.

The Outback – Pearl and Peril of Australia

Auf den Seiten 50 und 51 können die Schüler neben den interessanten Fotografien aus dem Outback erkennen, dass die wunderschöne Natur auch gefährliche Seiten hat. Touristen im Outback werden immer wieder aufgefordert, vorsichtig zu sein, genügend Wasser mit sich zu führen, sich möglichst nicht abseits der offiziellen Routen zu bewegen und, wenn sie schon eigene oder wenig befahrene und begangene Wege beschreiten wollen, sich vorher am nächsten Ziel anzumelden, damit sie im Falle ihres Ausbleibens gesucht werden können.
Die Fotocollage in Form einer Postkarte auf Seite 50 stellt die Thematik „Dürre und Wasser" in den Vordergrund. Im Bild links oben sind aufziehende Wolken und ein Sandsturm zu erkennen, rechts daneben ein Wasserlauf nach einem der selten eintretenden Regenfälle, unten links eine Windmühle zur Förderung von Grundwasser und daneben ein Salzsee, in dem sämtliches Wasser verdunstet ist. Im ovalen Bild in der Mitte sieht man eines der vielen toten Kängurus, die entlang der Hauptverkehrsadern durch das Outback (Stuart Highway, Lasseter Highway) durch Unfälle verendet sind.

I never knew this about Australia

Im gelben Informationskasten werden einige wesentliche Charakteristika des Outback zusammengefasst: Landschaftskriterien, Temperaturen, Flora und Fauna, Wirtschaft und Besiedlung. Mit diesen Daten kann auf verschiedene Weise gearbeitet werden. Entweder lesen alle Schüler den gesamten Text und eignen ihn sich als Hintergrundwissen an, um es bei der Beantwortung der Fragen in den *Activities* zu benutzen, oder die Lehrkraft verteilt die Abschnitte auf einige Schüler, die sich zum jeweiligen Thema anhand des vorgegebenen Textes und mithilfe weiterer Recherchen speziell vorbereiten und darüber vor der Klasse referieren.

Der grau unterlegte Text am Seitenrand ist ein Zitat aus der Informationsbroschüre des *Uluru-Kata Tjuta National Park*. Darin stellen sich die Eigentümer der Region um den *Ayers Rock*, die Anangu, vor. Im Jahr 1985 wurde diesem indigenen Volk nach langen Rechtsstreitigkeiten der von ihnen *Uluru* genannte Heilige Berg wieder als rechtmäßiges Eigentum zurückgegeben. Der Staat hat sich jedoch die Nutzung der Nationalparks und der Straßen dorthin vorbehalten. Das Besteigen des äußerst steilen *Uluru* wird von den *Anangu* ausdrücklich nicht gewünscht, ebenso das Fotografieren der heiligen Plätze dieser monolithischen Felsformation, die sich im Übrigen unterirdisch weiter erstreckt bis hin zu den *Kata Tjuta*, den *Olgas*. Manche Touristen respektieren diesen Wunsch der Eigentümer allerdings nicht. Das traurige Ergebnis (außer dieser Respektlosigkeit) sind trotz der vorhandenen Sicherungen jährlich wiederkehrende Unfälle und sogar Todesfälle.

Auf dem staatlich genutzten Gebiet ist die Einreise von Touristen ohne Weiteres möglich. Jegliches Abweichen von diesem Territorium in das Gebiet der *Anangu* hinein bedarf aber deren ausdrücklicher Genehmigung.

In der auf dem Seitenrand abgedruckten Begrüßung bitten die *Anangu* selbstbewusst darum, sie auch mit diesem Namen zu bezeichnen. Denn die von den britischen Eroberern geprägten verallgemeinernden Begriffe *„Aboriginals“* (dieser Begriff ist aber nicht mehr politisch korrekt) oder *„Indigenous people“* entsprechen nicht dem nationalen Selbstverständnis der verschiedenen Völker der Ureinwohner Australiens. Die allgemein als politisch korrekt erachtete Bezeichnung ist *Aborigine* bzw. *Aborigines*. In vielen Zusammenhängen (z. B. in den Kunstgattungen) wird auch offiziell jedoch das Adjektiv *Aboriginal* verwendet.

Bei der aus Platzgründen beschränkten Aufzählung der im Outback lebenden Tiere werden zum Beispiel die vor allem im 19. Jahrhundert als Transportmittel nach Australien eingeführten, aber später ausgewilderten Dromedare (*camels*) nicht erwähnt. Sie stellen in den letzten Jahren aufgrund ihrer kontinuierlichen Vermehrung eine wachsende Gefahr für die Natur und die Menschen dar, weil sie eine Nahrungskonkurrenz für Schafe und Rinder sind und auf der Suche nach Wasser sogar in Siedlungen eindringen. Regelmäßig werden deshalb Kamele eingefangen und verkauft. Im Jahr 2009 wurden von der Regierung sogar 19 Millionen Australische Dollar für ein Programm zum Abschießen der Tiere bewilligt.

Die ebenfalls ausgewilderten *brumbies* (Pferde) sind noch keine derartige Bedrohung. Eine andere Tierart aber, nämlich die in den 30er-Jahren des 20. Jahrhunderts zur Käferbekämpfung nach Australien gebrachten Aga-Kröten (Bufo marinus; engl. *cane toads*), erweisen sich als eine regelrechte Landplage. Sie fressen Insekten, Frösche, kleine Säugetiere, sogar Reptilien und Vögel. Dadurch bedrohen sie den Artenreichtum, darüber hinaus sind sie aber auch tödlich giftig für Mensch und Tier. Die Süßwasserkrokodile sind durch sie bereits stark dezimiert (2009). In manchen besonders stark befallenen Regionen werden deshalb Tausende Kröten gefangen und getötet. Ihre inzwischen auf viele Millionen geschätzte Population bedeutet trotzdem inzwischen eine Gefahr für das ökologische Gleichgewicht.

Solutions

Activities p. 52

1. **Name some of the characteristic features of the Outback.**
   The Outback covers about 80 % of Australia's total territory. It is characterized by an extremely hot and dry climate and rugged landscapes. The Northern Territory, which covers a big part of the Outback, is characterized by two distinctive climate zones: a tropical zone in the north and deserts in the centre and south. Across this vast region, agriculture is mainly limited to cattle, sheep and buffalo production, and in the north, to field crops, fruit and vegetables.

2. **What should tourists in the Outback pay special attention to?**
   Tourists should keep to the official routes. They should always carry enough water with them (5–10 litres per person per day, depending on the season and the region). All people should be extremely careful when walking across open country because there may be snakes, spiders and other poisonous animals. Swimming in pools and rivers is only recommended where it is officially allowed, because otherwise you may encounter crocodiles.

3. **Make sure you know these animals: kangaroo, wallaby, dingo, emu, gecko, eagle, kite. Design a poster containing facts about the Outback, including some of the animals living there.**
   Making a poster or producing a PowerPoint presentation is a good way for the students to learn more about the animals living in the Outback.

4. **Interpret the temperature map given above. What conclusions do you draw as to the quality of living in different regions of Australia?**
   In the given map, the respective temperatures are indicated by colours. The dominating yellow colour in the centre and on the west coast shows that there are temperatures of about 50 to 60 degrees Celsius in summer (December to February). Living in these areas is extremely hard or even impossible. On the other hand, the dark or light blue colours show moderate climate zones. These are located along the coasts of the continent, mainly on the east coast and partly along the north and south coasts. It is here that all larger settlements are to be found. More than 90 % of the total population of Australia lives in cities or towns, most of which are located on the east and south coasts.

The Making of Australia

In diesem Kapitel werden exemplarisch einige Kapitel der australischen Geschichte vorgestellt. Es geht nicht um eine lückenlose Aufzählung von Jahreszahlen, sondern um das Verständnis dafür, wie den Urvölkern des australischen Kontinents mit all ihren Jahrtausende alten Kulturen seit Beginn der Landnahme durch britische Eroberer und Siedler eine zweite Kultur übergestülpt wurde, unter deren Last die indigenen Traditionen fast ausgelöscht wurden.

The Rainbow Snake – Aboriginal Dreamtime Story

Die Mythologie der indigenen Völker Australiens und der Torres Strait Islands weist eine mit den unterschiedlichen Sprachen einhergehende große Diversität auf (siehe z. B. die Webseite http://en.wikipedia.org/wiki/Australian_Aboriginal_mythology). Die *dreamtime stories* oder kurz *Dreamtime* genannten mündlichen Überlieferungen basieren auf einem tiefen, mit der Natur untrennbar verbundenen Glauben. Sie sind den *Anangu, Pitjantjatjara, Ngaanyatjarra, Ngaatjatjarra* und den anderen uraustralischen Völkern ebenso heilig wie zum Beispiel der *Uluru* (*Ayers Rock*). Wenn trotzdem die mythischen Geschichten auch von *Aborigines* ins Netz gestellt werden, dann in der Regel mit der Bitte, sie zu lesen oder sich anzuhören, aber nicht mit anderen Medien zu verbreiten. Mit Rücksicht darauf wird in diesem Buch auf den Abdruck einer der vielen authentischen, von den indigenen Familien heute noch tradierten mythischen Geschichten verzichtet. Stattdessen wird gezeigt, wie sich Menschen in aller Welt mit der australischen Mythologie beschäftigen, hier am Beispiel einer Schule in Großbritannien. Schüler haben die Geschichte von der Regenbogenschlange nacherzählt und eine Illustration dazu im Stil des traditionellen *dot painting* der *Aborigines* geschaffen.
Im Kursunterricht können die Schüler diese und weitere *dreamtime stories* im Internet nachlesen, nacherzählen und sich mit ihrer künstlerischen Umsetzung auseinandersetzen.
Zu diesem Thema können die Schüler unter anderem die folgenden Webseiten lesen bzw. sich die Geschichten anhören: *dreamtime signs* (www.innovated.gov.au), *dreamtime stories told* (www.dreamtime.net.au) und *dot painting* (www.ohmsartgallery.com).

Solutions

Activities p. 54

1. **Retell the Dreamtime story in your own words.**
   Individual answers.

2. **Search the website www.dreamtime.net.au/dreaming/storylist.htm to read more Dreamtime stories and find out what role the Rainbow Snake and other characters play in Aboriginal mythology.**
   The students should understand that the Rainbow Snake and other characters play a dominant role in Aboriginal mythology. The Rainbow Snake personifies the basic conception that the Aboriginal people have of the birth of the Earth.

3. **Using the information given on pages 54 and 55, analyse the Australian Aboriginal spiritual beliefs and compare these to other versions of Creation mythology.**
   The Aboriginal belief system is deeply rooted in the close relationship between people and nature. According to their mythology, Heaven (represented by the Rain-

bow or Rainbow Snake) came to Earth to create all life and nature. In other myths of Creation, the Lord, Buddha or other gods created both the Earth und everything and everyone on it.
In multicultural classes, the students may belong to different confessions so that it could be possible to have them tell different Creation stories according to the holy texts of their religions.

I never knew this about Australia

In der gelben Box werden interessante Informationen über die Erstbesiedlung des australischen Kontinents, die Populationsentwicklung, *Dreamtime* und die frühe Kultur der indigenen Bevölkerung gegeben. Außerdem werden die Rolle der indigenen Kulturen im heutigen Australien sowie die Bedeutung der Flaggen der *Aboriginal people* und der *Torres Strait Islanders* kurz umrissen, die ebenfalls zur Urbevölkerung Australiens gehören, aber nicht auf dem Festland leben.
Außer der Lektüre dieser Infobox können die Schüler einige Bereiche selbstständig weiter recherchieren, z. B. über die Entwicklung der Bevölkerung bzw. die Geschichte der Flaggen, oder sich mit der Zeichensprache der Ureinwohner beschäftigen. Die sechs Beispiele am Seitenrand sind einem Arbeitsblatt für die Besucher des *National Museum of Australia* (Canberra) entnommen, ebenso wie die Abbildungen im **Worksheet 5**. Sie gehören der Zeichensprache der *Papunja* an und werden bis zum heutigen Tage vor allem im Kunstschaffen der *Indigenous people* benutzt. Das Arbeitsblatt kann die Schüler in einer *hands-on activity* näher an die volkstümliche Ausdrucksweise der australischen Ureinwohner heranführen.

A Nation is Born

In einem kurzen Text werden die zwei bedeutendsten Entdecker Australiens vorgestellt: Willem Janszoon (ca. 1570–1630) und James Cook (1728–1779). Daraus erfahren die Schüler nach dem Prinzip der Lernspirale wieder etwas mehr über die Geschichte des Landes. Fächerübergreifend kann die Klasse gemeinsam mit den Lehrkräften für Geografie und/oder Geschichte auch weiter über diese beiden Persönlichkeiten recherchieren. Im Text wird auch das Schicksal der ersten Sträflinge (*convicts*) angedeutet, deren Nachkommen heute noch in Australien leben. Angesichts der Vielzahl von späteren Einwanderern wird man in Australien allerdings nur selten wirklich jemandem begegnen, der stolz von sich behauptet: *One of my ancestors was a convict.*

Solutions

Activities p. 56

1. **What are Willem Janszoon and James Cook famous for? Give a rough idea of how they contributed to Australian history.**
   Willem Janszoon was a Dutch explorer who is the first European known to have seen the coast of Australia in 1606. By charting some 320 km of the coastline (albeit in the belief that it was a southerly extension of New Guinea), he laid the foundation stone for all further exploration of Australia.
   In 1770, Captain James Cook claimed the east coast of Australia for the British Crown. This opened the way for Britain to later use this land as a penal colony, which formed the beginning of British settlement in Australia.

2. **Compare Australia's development in the 19th century with the history of Europe and the United States of America at the same time. Draw three historical timelines, and fill in the most important economic, political and social events on these continents.**
The students might, for example, put the history timelines into a grid like that on **Worksheet 6**. The students could also use the three timelines given in the grid to talk about world history in the 19th century.

3. **Most people have come to Australia as immigrants. Just a few will proudly confess that their great-grandfathers were convicts. Given these different paths, who really is a 'True Blue Australian'? Is it the Indigenous people, or first, second, third generation immigrants? Or is it everybody who embraces the culture and lifestyle of Australia and chooses to be a citizen? Discuss and judge for yourself.**
The term "true blue Australian" is a phrase used to describe people who are "real" Australians. Doing this task not only offers the students the chance to discuss who is truly Australian, but also to consider who is a "real" German. In this discussion, the term multiculturalism and what this entails will also play a bigger role.

4. **Write an essay on the topic "Who is German?"**
The ideas for an essay on this topic will arise naturally from the discussion before. The teacher may want to grade the students' papers.

Stolen

Jane Harrison

Parallel zum Kursbuch „Australia and New Zealand“ sollten die Schüler möglichst auch mehrere Kurzgeschichten und eine Ganzschrift zu diesem Thema lesen. Das beeindruckende Theaterstück „Stolen“ ist eine hierfür sehr geeignete Lektüre. Der abgedruckte Ausschnitt stammt aus einer broschierten Ausgabe (Jane Harrison: Stolen, Langenscheidt Verlag, Berlin 2005, S. 540–541). Darin verarbeitet die Autorin, selbst eine Aborigine vom Stamm der *Muruwari* in New South Wales bei Bourke, das noch heute die australische Gesellschaft belastende Erbe der *stolen generations*. Als in den 20er Jahren des 20. Jahrhunderts deutlich wurde, das die indigenen Völker trotz ihrer Unterdrückung durch die weißen Einwanderer weiter bestehen und sich entwickeln würden, fasste die australische Regierung einen Beschluss, nach dem alle Aborigines Teile des australischen Mainstream, also in die australische Gesellschaft einbezogen werden sollten. Dazu begann man, die indigenen Kinder gewaltsam ihren Eltern und ihrer heimischen Umgebung zu entreißen und sie in Heimen „umzuerziehen“. Diese noch bis weit in die zweite Hälfte des 20. Jahrhunderts reichende Praxis hinterließ starke psychische Schäden bei den Betroffenen und spaltete schließlich sogar die „weiße“ Gesellschaft. Erst 2007 war die Zeit dafür reif, dass sich der neu gewählte Premierminister Kevin Rudd sich öffentlich für die Misshandlung der Ureinwohner des Landes entschuldigte (s. auch das nächste Kapitel).
Ein anderes Drama, in dessen Dialogen das Los der *Aborigines* und ihr Leiden unter den weißen Eroberern deutlich werden, ist das Schauspiel „No sugar“ von Jack Davis. Zur Ergänzung der Thematik kann der Ausschnitt daraus in **Worksheet 7** gelesen und besprochen werden.

Solutions

Activities p. 57

1. **Bearing in mind what was said about the 'Stolen Generations' on page 55, analyse the situation in the play. What feelings do the protagonist and her parents reveal?**

How did the problem come about? What solution to the problem do you see? Discuss.

Anne's parents have always only wanted the best for their daughter. That is why they did not tell her that her biological mother was an Aboriginal lady. They think it was justifiable not to have informed their daughter before, because they were worried that Anne's being of Aboriginal descent might have led to discrimination.
Anne herself is deeply confused and angry when she hears this. She is of the opinion that her parents should have told her about her mother before. She thinks her parents should be ashamed of their behaviour.
The problem came about when Anne's biological mother was dying. Only then were her adoptive parents no longer able to stand the fact that they had not told their daughter the whole truth.
Answers will vary. However, the students will most probably discuss questions of trust and love between parents and their children.

2. **Imagine you are Anne. Write her diary entry for this day.**
A diary entry is mostly short and often uses individual abbreviations. The students can decide whether they wish to write in complete sentences or just make notes. Regardless which form of writing the students choose, they should subsequently tell the class about their diary entry.

The Burnum Burnum Declaration

Burnum Burnum

Im langen Kampf der Ureinwohner und einiger weißer Aktivisten für ihre Rechte haben sich einige Persönlichkeiten besonders hervorgetan. Unter ihnen ist vor allem Burnum Burnum (1936–1997) zu nennen, *„activist, rugby player, actor, author, dreamer and respected Aboriginal elder“* (Macquarie PEN Anthology of Aboriginal Literature).
Burnum Burnum wurde Harry Penrith getauft, nahm aber später den Namen seines Urgroßvaters an, der *Great Warrior* bedeutet. Er erregte große Aufmerksamkeit mit seiner bissig-satirischen „Declaration“, in der er die gesamte Geschichte Australiens in den letzten 200 Jahren umkehrt: Die Urbevölkerung Australiens erklärt England zu ihrem Besitz. Die Bewohner Australiens versprechen aber, den weißen Einwohnern Großbritanniens keinen Schaden zufügen zu wollen und werden schließlich nach 200 Jahren Oberherrschaft einen Vertrag abschließen, der die Eroberung auf friedlichem Wege rechtsgültig macht.
Der Text der Erklärung enthält beinahe in jeder Wendung eine satirische Verfremdung der tatsächlichen Verhältnisse. Dies erschwert das Verständnis, überhöht andererseits aber auch die politische Aussage und macht zum Dritten den literarischen Genuss bei der Lektüre aus. Aus den genannten Gründen sollte der Text sehr gründlich mit dem Wörterbuch gelesen und besprochen, in Teilen vielleicht sogar übersetzt werden.

Solutions

1. **What does Burnum Burnum declare? What is the author's intention? Comment on the text.** Activities p. 58
Burnum Burnum, appointing himself as a nobleman of ancient Australia, declares England to now be a possession of the Aboriginal people. Nevertheless, he promises not to harm the native population of England. For example, he pledges not to sterilize English women, nor to separate their children from their families. Instead, he promises to bring them good manners and to educate them according to Abo-

riginal traditions. He also plans to offer the more advanced Englishmen the chance to learn his Pitjantjatjara language. He assures the English that he will then make a treaty in two hundred years time to validate the occupation of their country by peaceful means. He also solemnly promises not to exploit England's raw materials or export them to Australia, and never to destroy England's natural environment, but on the contrary, to instead unite all people of both nations in a common, productive peaceful purpose.
Burnum Burnum uses satire to unmask, after almost 200 years, the merciless supression and exploitation of the Indigenous people by the British invaders.
In their comments on the text, the students should show that they understand both the satirical character of the Declaration and the author's true intentions.

2. **Analyse the stylistic devices the author uses. Give examples.**
The main stylistic device the use of satire and irony. Every single statement of the "Declaration" must be converted to its opposite to properly understand the accusations that Burnum Burnum is making against the British conquerors of Australia.
Another stylistic device used at the beginning of the text is the introduction "I, Burnum Burnum, being a nobleman of ancient Australia do hereby take possession of England on behalf of the Aboriginal People." This establishes a very official and hence trustworthy impression, and the use of different facts and figures further adds to this impression.
In addition, the form of the text has been carefully chosen. In many ways, it resembles a contract, which thus underlines its importance, or alternatively, it could be seen as a description of the status quo, which could in fact frighten the British reader when reading it.

The Great Ocean Road – A Symbol of National Identity

Die fast 250 km lange *Great Ocean Road* entlang der Südküste Australiens wurde (auch als Arbeitsbeschaffungsmaßnahme) zwischen 1919 und 1932 von Heimkehrern aus dem Ersten Weltkrieg erbaut. Dieses enorme Projekt diente dazu, die Bevölkerung der Ostküste und die der Westküste mithilfe einer schnellen Verbindungsstraße einander näher zu bringen. Nach der eben erst (1901) erfolgten Gründung des *Commonwealth of Australia* und dem furchtbaren Erleben des Krieges, in dem das *Australian and New Zealand Army Corps (ANZAC)* große Verluste nicht nur bei Gallipoli zu beklagen hatte, war dieses Bauvorhaben das erste große positive gemeinsame Werk der Australier, das sie erst richtig zu einer Nation verschweißte.

Solutions

Activities p. 59

1. **Describe the pictures. What natural beauties do they show?**
The Great Ocean Road is rich in beautiful landscapes and home to many interesting animals. Among the many famous sights along this stretch of road are the so-called "Twelve Apostles" which were given their name in 1950. The distinctive shapes of these limestone rock formations, which are scattered along the coast of Victoria, have been formed by wind and water erosion. However, these processes are also leading, one by one, to their eventual destruction. In June 2009, another one of them, Island Archway, shown in the picture, collapsed into the sea and thus lost its arch. In 2010, there just remained eight "Apostles".

Australia boasts more than 800 species of eucalyptus trees. Eucalyptus woods are a beautiful part of Australia's nature and the habitat of koalas, red kangaroos, wallabies, emus, wombats and lots of other animals. (A very interesting site about koalas is www.koalahospital.org.au.)
The ocean is also home to many animals including fairy penguins (shown top middle), whales, sharks; jellyfish and many other forms of sealife.
The beautiful landscapes, flora and fauna along the Great Ocean Road attract thousands of tourists from Australia and abroad every year as, for example, the backpackers in front of their van, shown middle left.

2. **Search the web to find out who built the Great Ocean Road, why it became a symbol of national identity, and why it attracts thousands of tourists every year. Prepare a presentation.**
   Individual answers. The students can work in groups or individually. One result of their work could be a summary poster on the Great Ocean Road.

Worksheet 5

Papunja Painting

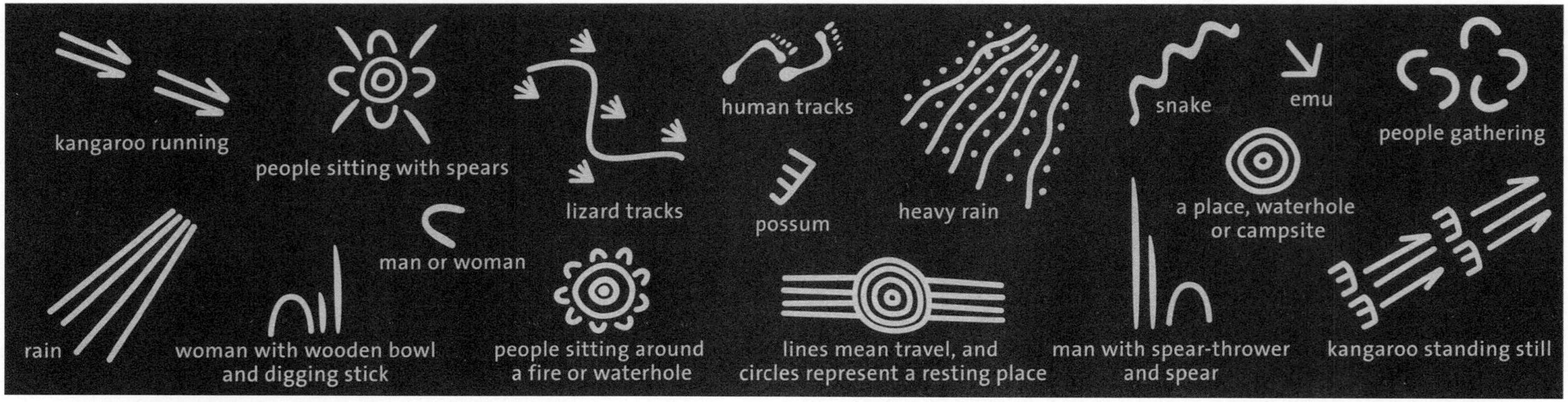

Try to copy these symbols.

Worksheet 6

History Timelines of Australia, the USA and Europe for the 19th century (example)

Australia	USA	Europe
1813 Matthew Flinders changes New South Wales (Australia's old name) to Australia	**1803** Louisiana Purchase Treaty	**1800** Social reforms in Scotland (Robert Owen)
1817 Australia's first bank opens in Sydney (it became Westpac in 1982)	**1808** U.S. slave trade with Africa ends	**1801** Ireland united with Great Britain
1824 A penal colony is founded at Moreton Bay (now the city of Brisbane)	**1823** Monroe Doctrine	**1804** Napoleon crowns himself Emperor of France
1829 The whole of Australia is claimed as British territory	**1830** Indian Removal Act	**1805** "Fidelio" by L. van Beethoven is first performed in Vienna
1835 J. Batman and J. P. Fawkner establish a settlement at Port Phillip (now Melbourne)	**1832** Black Hawk War	**1806** Napoleon defeats Russians and Austrians at Austerlitz; the Holy Roman Empire is formally ended
1841 New Zealand proclaimed as a separate colony, no longer part of New South Wales	**1836** Creek War	**1808** Goethe's "Faust I" is first published
1842 Copper discovered in South Australia	**1845** Texas Annexation	**1812** Napoleon invades Russia; Napoleonic Empire begins to collapse
1850 Western Australia becomes a penal colony; Australia's first university founded: the University of Sydney	**1846** U.S.-Mexican War begins	**1813** Prussia begins War of Liberation against France
1851 Victorian Gold Rush starts	**1848** California Gold Rush begins	**1815** Napoleon is defeated at Waterloo; Congress of Vienna
1858 Sydney and Melbourne linked by electric telegraph	**1861** Confederate States of America established; Civil War begins	**1824** British trade unions form
1867 Gold discovered in Queensland	**1862** Pacific Railway Act	**1831** Faraday discovers electromagnetic induction
1868 Transportation of convicts to Western Australia ceases	**1862** General Robert E. Lee serves as commander of the Confederate Army	**1833** Slavery abolished in the British Empire
1869 Removal of children of Australian Aboriginal and Torres Strait Islander descent from their parents begins	**1863** Battle of Gettysburg	**1834** Civil War begins in Spain
1872 Telegraph line linking Darwin and Adelaide opens	**1864** National Banking Act	**1838** First transatlantic steamboat crossings between the USA and Britain
1873 Uluru first sighted by Europeans	**1865** Assassination of Abraham Lincoln	**1844** Utopian socialism becomes popular
1879 First congress of trade unions held	**1866** Civil Rights Act; Ku Klux Klan founded	**1845** Potato crop fails throughout Europe, Ireland is the hardest hit, massive migration to the USA
1880 The bushranger Ned Kelly hanged	**1867** Alaska Purchase from Russia	**1848** Beginning of the Revolutions of 1848 in the German states
	1868 University of California founded	**1854** Crimean War begins in Europe
	1870 First graduate programmes at Yale and Harvard	
	1871 Great Chicago Fire	
	1871 Treaty of Washington with the British Empire regarding Canada	
	1872 Yellowstone National Park created	
	1875 Civil Rights Act	
	1876 National League of baseball founded; Battle of Little Bighorn; Graham Bell invents the telephone	
	1879 Thomas A. Edison invents the light bulb	
	1881 Clara Barton creates the Red Cross	

Worksheet 6

Australia	USA	Europe
1889 Completion of the railway network between Adelaide, Brisbane, Melbourne and Sydney **1891** The Convention adopts the federal constitution **1891** Severe economic depression hits Australia **1892** Gold is discovered in Western Australia **1894** South Australia becomes the second place in the world to grant women's suffrage **1895** Waltzing Matilda is first sung in public **1901** The Commonwealth of Australia is founded	**1888** National Geographic Society founded **1890** Yosemite National Park founded **1896** Gold discovered in the Yukon's Klondike **1896** Hawaii annexed **1897** Boston subway completed	**1856** Invention of Henry Bessemer's converter which revolutionizes steel production **1859** Charles Darwin publishes "On the Origin of Species" **1861** Slavery in Russia is abolished **1864** First International (a network of influential trade unions in Britain and France) founded in London **1867** Austro-Hungarian dual monarchy established **1871** The United German Empire is declared; the Paris Commune is established **1877** Russia declares war on Turkey **1879** Britain declares war on the Zulus in South Africa **1884** Social reforms continue under Bismarck in Germany **1885** Karl Benz invents the automobile **1893** Art Nouveau becomes dominant throughout Europe **1896** Baron Coubertin revives Olympic Games **1898** Russian scientist Konstantin Tsiolkovsky provides the theoretical basis for space travel **1900** The so-called Boxer Rebellion in China begins

Worksheet 7

"No Sugar"

Jack Davis

Aboriginal history has found manifold reflection in works of art. Below is a scene from Jack Davis's play "No sugar" (Act 2, scene 6). Some indigenous men are talking around a campfire. They speak non-standard English and slang mixed with words from their native language Noongar.

BILLY: This country got plenty good dance, eh?
BLUEY: *Wee-ah!*
JIMMY: Ah, *yuart,* not too many left now. Nearly all finish.
BILLY: No, no, no. You song man, you fella[1] dance men. This still your country (*Flinging his arms wide*) You, you, you, you listen! *Gudeeah*[2] make 'em fences, windmill, make 'em road for motor car, big house, cut 'em down trees. Still your country! Not like my country, finish ... finish. (*He sits in silence. They watch him intently. JOE puts wood on the fire. He speaks slowly.*)
BILLY: Kuliyah. (*Miming pulling a trigger*[3], *grunting*) Gudeeah bin kill 'em. Finish, kill 'em. Big mob, 1926, kill 'em big mob my country.
SAM: Nietjuk?
BILLY: I bin stop Liveringa station and my brother, he bin run from Oombulgarri[4]. (*Holding up four fingers.*) That many days. Night time too. He bin tell me 'bout them *gudeeah.* They bin two, three stockman *gudeeah.* Bin stop along that place, Juada Station, and this one *gudeeah* Midja George, he was riding and he come to this river and he see these two old womans, koories[5], there in the water hole. He says, what you doin' here? They say they gettin' gugja. (*He mimes pulling lily roots and eating.*) Midja George say, where the mans? They over by that tree sleepin', and Midja George, he get off his horse, and he bin belt[6] that old man with the stockwhip. He bin flog 'em, flog 'em, till that *gudeeah,* he get tired. Then he break the bottle glass spear, and he break the *chubel*[7] spear. (*He grunts and mimes this.*) And that old man, he was bleedin', bleedin' from the eyes, and he get up and he pick up that one *chubel* spear, and he spear that one Midja George. (*He demonstrates violently.*) And that *gudeeah,* he get on his horse, he go little bit way and he fall off ... finish ... dead.
JIMMY: Serve the bastard right.
BILLY: No, no, no, bad for my mob. Real bad. That old man and his two koories, they do this next day. (*He indicates running away.*) Two *gudeeah* come looking for Midja George. They bin find him dead. (*Silence.*) (*Holding up a hand*) Must be that many day. Big mob *gudeeah.* Big mob politjmans, and big mob from stations, and shoot 'em everybody mens, *koories,* little *yumbah*[8]. (*He grunts and mimes pulling a trigger.*) They chuck 'em on a big fire, chuck[9] 'em in river. (*They sit in silence, mesmerized and shocked by* BILLY'S *gruesome*[10] *story.*)

Jack Davis: "No Sugar", Currency Press, Michigan 1986

[1] **fella** fellow [2] **gudeeah** white person [3] **trigger** *Abzug (einer Waffe)* [4] **Oombulgarri** a place name [5] **koorie** Aboriginal word for themselves (used mainly in N.S.W.) [6] **to belt** to hit [7] **chubel** spear [8] **yumbah** children [9] **to chuck** to throw [10] **gruesome** shocking, cruel

Politics and Economy

Das *Commonwealth of Australia* wurde 1901 als parlamentarische Demokratie gegründet. Zugleich stellt es eine konstitutionelle Monarchie dar, da der König oder die Königin Großbritanniens (seit 1952 ist dies Queen Elizabeth II.) das Staatsoberhaupt (*Head of State*) Australiens ist. In diesem Kapitel werden die Politik und Wirtschaft des Landes mit besonderem Bezug auf das 20. Jahrhundert anhand ausgewählter authentischer Texte und eines Flussdiagramms beschrieben.

The Nation Apologises

Der erste Text ist der Beginn der historischen *Sorry Speech* von Premierminister Kevin Rudd im Februar 2007. Diese Rede geht auf die den Ureinwohnern Australiens im Verlauf der letzten 200 Jahre zugefügten Leiden ein. Die Schüler können sich die Parlamentsrede im Text durchlesen, aber auch unabhängig davon oder zugleich im Internet anhören (s. Aufgabe 2).

Solutions

Activities p. 60

1. **What does the Australian government have to say sorry for? Make a list.**
   Kevin Rudd apologises for
   – the mistreatment of the indigenous peoples in the past,
   – the mistreatment of the so-called "stolen generations", especially for the removal of Aboriginal and Torres Strait Islander children from their families,
   – all the laws that have caused his fellow Australians great suffering.
   The students may just name the single issues or could be asked to explain them in more detail.

2. **Watch the video clip for more information on the speech: www.smh.com.au/multimedia/2008/national/australia-says-sorry/main.html. Take notes on the speech, and give an oral summary.**
   Taking notes is a skill that will be necessary for the students in their further studies. Therefore, the teacher should urge them to practise it.
   On this website, there is a transcript of the entire "Sorry Speech": www.smh.com.au/articles/2008/02/13/1202760379056.html.

I Am Proud

Oodgeroo Noonuccal

Im Gedicht von Kathleen Jane Mary Ruska (1920–1993; verheiratete Walker; Pseudonym Oodgeroo Noonuccal nach dem Stamm, in dem sie geboren wurde) kommt der Nationalstolz aller *indigenous people* ebenso deutlich zum Ausdruck wie in der „Erklärung" von Burnum Burnum (s. das Kapitel „The Making of Australia"). Kath Walker bedient sich nur ganz anderer Mittel. Sie kontrastiert die schwarzhäutige Urbevölkerung mit den weißen Eroberern und bedient sich klarer Metaphern, in denen sie den vergebens geführten Kampf der *Aborigines* schildert und deutlich macht, dass alle Unterdrückung nicht den Stolz ihrer Landsleute brechen konnte. Eine Kurzbiographie der promovierten Schriftstellerin und Verfechterin der Rechte der indigenen Völker ist zu finden unter www.britannica.com/women/article-9104966.

Solutions

Activities p. 61

1. **Read the poem, and then consider who the speaker in the poem is, and how the person describes life.**
   There are two speakers in the poem: "I" is a single black Aborigine who tells us about himself or herself as an example of all indigenous people in Australia. "We" expresses the collective opinion of the Aboriginal peoples.
   In the poem, there is a first-person singular narrator who describes himself (or herself?) as being black but proud, broken, poor and dressed in rags but not ashamed of this.
   The first-person plural narrators who speak in the second part of the poem look back at their history and their fight against the white conquerors. They emphasize that, although they were conquered and compelled, they never became subservient or servile.

2. **Read the poem again. This time, pay special attention to the adjectives and verbs the author uses. Which feelings do they reflect?**
   In her poem, the author uses the following adjectives: black, white, broken, poor, humble, not ashamed, never subservient, never servile, proud.
   The first two adjectives reflect the clash of the two cultures in Australia. The next three adjectives (broken, poor, humble) describe Aboriginal life and living conditions. The last four adjectives clearly reflect the positive feelings of the Indigenous people towards their life and country.

3. **Recite the poem. Try to read it out with expression and emotion.**
   Reciting poems with expression helps students to better understand them. The teacher should even try to get some of the students to learn the poem by heart.

4. **Compare Oodgeroo Noonuccal's poem to Burnum Burnum's 'Declaration' (p. 58). Both are Aboriginal-born people. What feelings do they reveal, and what are their messages? Discuss.**
   Both texts reflect anger and resentment but also the pride of the Aboriginal peoples in their country and culture. The aim of Burnum Burnum's "Declaration" is obviously to change the situation by highlighting the injustices of it and simply to return the country and their rights to the Indigenous people. Oodgeroo Noonuccal simply describes the situation as it is and emphasizes the unchanged pride of her people. At the end of her poem, she compares the fate of her people with that of Jesus Christ: "Though humble and poor and without a home ... So was Christ." This builds a bridge from ancient Aboriginal myths to the modern Christianized society.
   To get the discussion started, two students could first give statements about both the "Declaration" and the "Poem" so that the class can react to them.

Australia's Government

Die Regierungsform Australiens basiert im Wesentlichen auf den Prinzipien des Föderalismus und der Gewaltenteilung. Die australische Regierung hat angesichts ihrer Geschichte manche Merkmale gemeinsam mit dem britischen politischen System, andere aber auch mit dem der USA oder anderen demokratischen Staaten, z. B. ein *House of Representatives* und einen *Senate*. Der internationale Vergleich der politischen Systeme kann einen Teil der Beschäftigung mit dem Aufbau der australischen Regierung ausmachen. Auch denkbar ist, dass die Klasse weitere Recherchen zu den in diesem Text genannten Personen anstellt und eine Präsentation daraus ableitet.

Solutions

Activities p. 62

1. **Explain why Australia is a parliamentary and constitutional monarchy.**
   Australia can be called a parliamentary monarchy as the Parliament is at the very heart of the national government, and the Queen of Great Britain is the official Head of State. The Parliament consists of the Queen (represented by the Governor-General), the Senate and the House of Representatives. These three elements make Australia a constitutional monarchy and parliamentary democracy.
2. **What are the different functions of Parliament, the Prime Minister and the Head of State in Australia? Explain.**
   To explain the different functions of the Prime Minister and the Head of State in more detail, the students should search the Internet for more information. The text on page 62 explains that the Head of State does not play a day-to-day role in Australian Government but appoints her representative in Australia who is called Governor-General. The Prime Minister leads the Government's everyday work.
3. **To understand the structure of Australia's government better, draw a mindmap or flowchart. Then give a talk on how this government works.**
   The flowchart on **Worksheet 8** can be shown just as an example; the students could, however, also use it to tell the class about the Australian government. Another example of a flowchart can be found on the website http://en.wikipedia.org/wiki/Government_of_Australia, which describes the legislative process in Australia.

Politics and Economy in the 20th Century

Die Broschüre für Einwanderer „Becoming an Australian Citizen", aus der der Text auf der Seite 63 zusammengestellt wurde, umreißt in wenigen Sätzen die politische und wirtschaftliche Geschichte des Landes. Die im Text genannten und einige weitere Parteien werden am Seitenrand aufgeführt. Wenn Interesse daran besteht, können die Schüler die einzelnen Parteien im Internet heraussuchen und ausführlichere Informationen zusammentragen. Eine Kurzbeschreibung der politisch bedeutendsten australischen Parteien wird im **Worksheet 9** gegeben. Dieses Arbeitsblatt kann alternativ anstelle eigener Recherchen der Schüler eingesetzt werden.

Australia – Neither Down nor Under

Der lexikalisch ein wenig schwierigere Text auf Seite 64 kann als Vorlesetext (Zahlen!) oder als mediatorische Übung eingesetzt werden. Die Illustrationen und der authentische Wirtschaftsbericht auf dieser Seite geben einen kurzen Abriss von der Wirtschaft Australiens. Wenn die Lehrkraft die Zeit und die Absicht hat, auf das Thema Wirtschaft näher einzugehen, dann könnte zum Beispiel die Energiewirtschaft näher betrachtet werden. Australien bezieht etwa 80 Prozent seiner Energie aus Kohlekraftwerken, was eine bedeutende Umweltverschmutzung mit sich bringt. Der 2009 von Premierminister Kevin Rudd eingebrachte Vorschlag, die Treibhausgasemission bis 2020 um 5 bis 25 Prozent zu reduzieren, ist im Parlament von den Grünen (denen das Programm nicht

weit genug ging) und von den Liberalen (die um die Arbeitsplätze fürchteten) abgelehnt worden. Unter anderem ist, wenn der CO_2-Ausstoß nicht drastisch reduziert und dem Klimawandel in Australien nicht ernsthaft entgegengewirkt wird, zum Beispiel das Great Barrier Reef in seiner Existenz bedroht. Dies würde neben einem unwiederbringlichen Verlust für das Weltnaturerbe ein milliardenschweres Minus in den Einnahmen aus dem weltweiten Tourismus dorthin bedeuten.
Das erste Bild oben (German backpacker) kann Anlass geben zu einem Unterrichtsgespräch darüber, welche Möglichkeiten bestehen, für eine längere Zeit am Programm „Work and Travel" in Australien teilzunehmen. Internetseiten hierzu sind rasch zu finden. Die Ergebnisse dieser Recherchen lassen sich mündlich oder auch schriftlich zusammenfassen. Die drei weiteren Fotografien illustrieren das Thema „Wirtschaft".

Solutions

Activities p. 64

1. **How did Australia develop politically and economically in the 19th and 20th centuries, and what are its economic strengths today? Describe in your own words.**
Example:
Measured in terms of its gross domestic product, Australia belongs to the world's most highly developed countries. Prior to the world financial crisis starting in 2008, the country had enjoyed a very long period of uninterrupted growth.
Australia has a free market capitalist system similar to that in most other Western countries. On the world market, it exports mainly gas, coal, iron and other raw materials, but is also known for its export of meat and food products. These agricultural and mining exports make up about 65 % of Australia's total exports. The main export partners are Asian countries and the United States of America. One of the main import partners is Germany.
Although the country has a positive trade balance, it has a relatively high current account deficit of 5.8 % in 2009, which according to the International Monetary Fund, is expected to grow even further over the next few years. Traditionally, Australia's economy has been closely linked with Europe and the USA; however, it is becoming more and more dependent on Asia, especially Japan and China.

2. **Using the data given in the text above and searching the web, create a statistical chart in which you compare Australia to other countries.**
The students should feel free to decide which form of graphic illustration they want to use. An interesting figure to compare with is the Gross Domestic Product (GDP) of the European Union: US$ 13,620,000,000,000.
Table: GDP (in US$) of the 16 leading countries in 2007 (extract)

Rank	Country	GDP (nominal)
1	United States of America	13,220,000,000,000
2	Japan	4,911,000,000,000
3	Germany	2,858,000,000,000
4	China	2,512,000,000,000
5	United Kingdom	2,341,000,000,000
8	Canada	1,089,000,000,000
11	South Korea	768,500,000,000
13	Russia	733,000,000,000
14	Australia	645,300,000,000
15	Brazil	620,700,000,000
16	The Netherlands	612,700,000,000

Data source: 2007 CIA World Factbook

Graph: Gross Domestic Product (in billion US$) of the 16 leading countries in 2007 (extract)

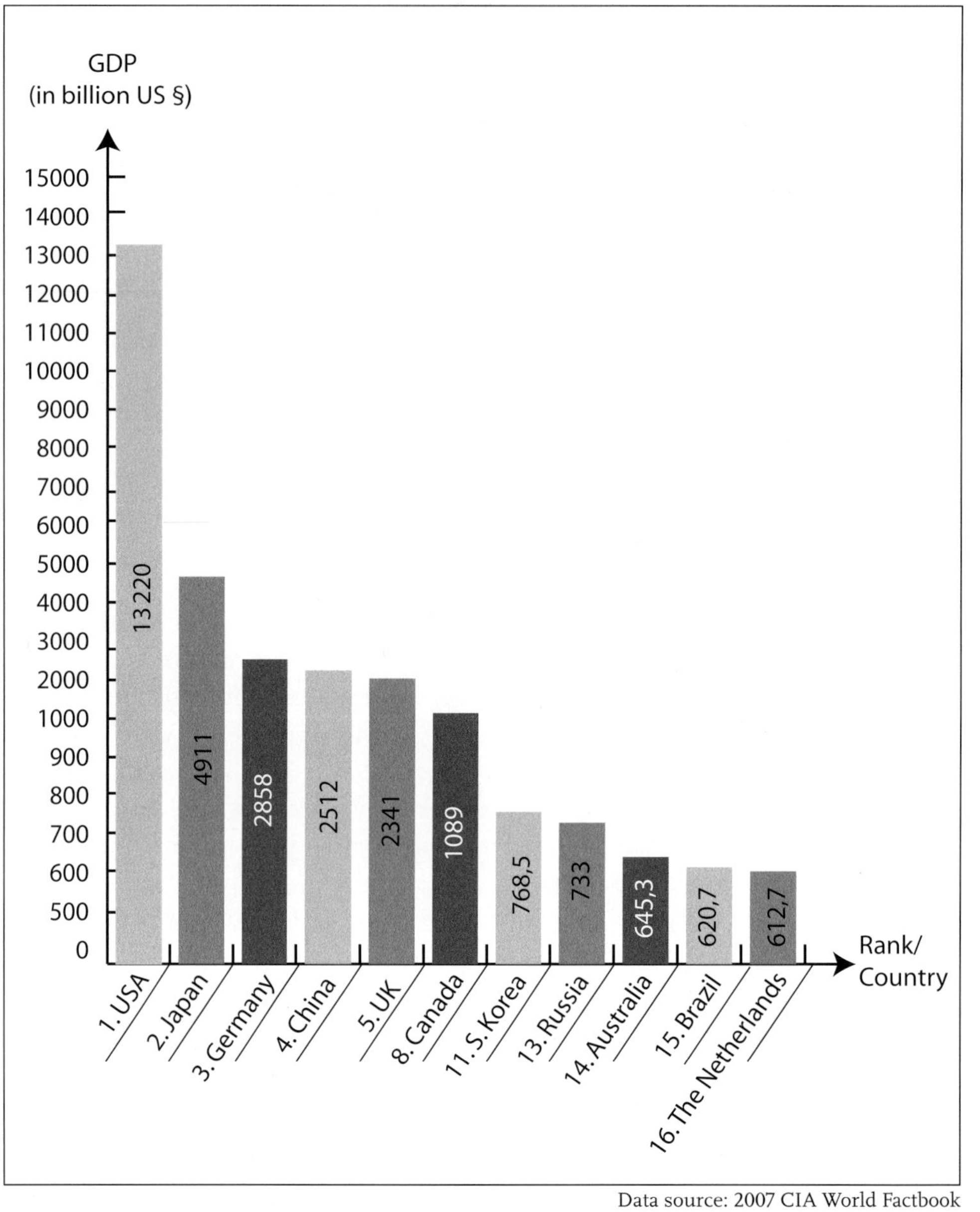

Data source: 2007 CIA World Factbook

3. **Read the texts on pp. 63 and 64 and search the web for more information on Australia's politics and economy. Give a presentation.**
   This presentation rounds up the reading and writing about Australia's economy. The students should become more and more used to giving longer presentations (about 15 to 30 minutes). This means that the summary presentation on Australia's economy should be given by one student or a small group of students.

Australia Quiz

Den Abschluss des ersten Teils des Kurses „Australia and New Zealand" kann das Wissensquiz über Australien bilden (s. **Worksheet 10**). Die Lehrkraft kopiert es entweder unverändert und lässt es die Schüler bearbeiten. Die Schüler können aber auch jeder bzw. jede für sich ein eigenes Quiz entwickeln und es einem Partner zum Raten übergeben. Die erste Variante berücksichtigt den behandelten Kurs insgesamt und ist wenig arbeitsaufwändig, die zweite lässt die Schüler aktiv werden und macht es möglich, den tatsächlich behandelten Stoff genauer zu berücksichtigen, ist aber zeit- und arbeitsintensiv. In beiden Fällen wird das spielerische Moment unterstrichen und die Motivation der Kursgruppe erhöht, wenn Preise für die meisten richtigen Antworten in Aussicht gestellt werden.

Worksheet 8

Australian Government

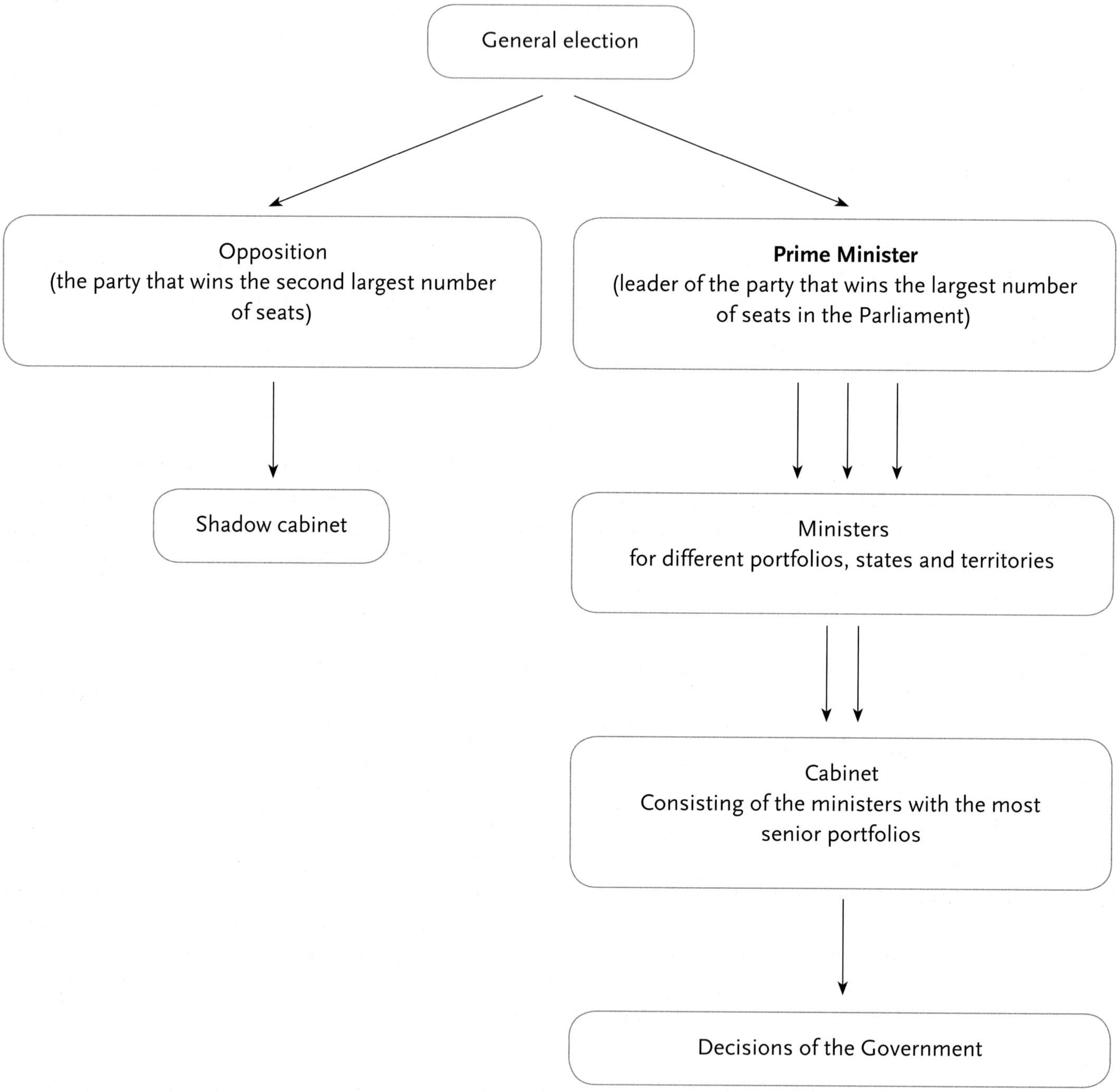

Worksheet 9

Political Parties in Australia

Australian Labor Party
The ALP is Australia's oldest political party, formed in the 1890s and is the only party to have been continuously represented in the House of Representatives since 1901. In the twentieth century, it experienced three debilitating splits, which kept it out of office for many years. Overall, it has governed federally for about one-third of the years since Federation, with the greatest portion of these between 1983–96, under Bob Hawke and Paul Keating. After three successive terms under the Liberal government of John Howard, Kevin Rudd (Australia's 26th Prime Minister) finally led the ALP back into power in 2007. In June 2010, Julia Gillard become Australia's first woman prime minister.

Liberal Party
Originally formed from a merger of the Protectionist and Free Trade parties in 1910, the Liberal Party has undergone several reformations, culminating in the present-day party that was formed by its iconic founder, Robert Menzies. Menzies governed from 1939–1941 and for 16 years from 1949 and is Australia's longest-serving prime minister. However, more recently, the Liberal Party had a long run of success with John Howard as their leader (1996–2007).

The Nationals
Originally known as the Country Party, this party has held seats in the federal parliament since 1919, changing its name to the National Country Party in the 1970s, then to the National Party in the 1980s, and finally to The Nationals in 2003. From 1996–2007, they governed in coalition with the Liberal Party, but over the past few years, this rural-based party has seen a steady decline in its voter support base as regional voters have become increasingly disillusioned with their representation at state and federal levels.

Australian Democrats
Formed in 1977 by a disaffected former Liberal party member Don Chipp, the Australian Democrats is the most successful minor political party in Australian history. Although it has never won a House of Representatives seat, since 1981 it has continually held or shared the balance of power in the Senate. It is also the only party to have elected not one, but five different women as leader. In recent years, the party has suffered a debilitating internal split, Natasha Stott Despoja's departure from the leadership and plummeting opinion poll ratings. Its future is therefore problematic.

Australian Greens
The Australian Greens Party was initially a phenomenon of the 1980s, arising out of a number of environmental battles of that time, such as the fight to save the Franklin Dam in Tasmania; however the official launch as a national party was not until 1992. From 1989–1992, five Greens held the balance of power in Tasmania's state parliament, and during the early 1990s, the Greens also attracted strong support in Western Australia. By 2005, there were four Greens senators in Federal Parliament, including their party leader Bob Brown.

One Nation
Formed by a disendorsed and disenchanted Liberal Party candidate, Pauline Hanson, in 1996, One Nation rose to prominence in Queensland in the 1998 state election when it won 11 seats in parliament. It followed this by winning a Queensland Senate seat in 1998 and polling 8.43 % of the primary vote in the House of Representatives, making it the third largest party in terms of voter support at that time. The party quickly went into decline amid internal bickering, eventually lost its parliamentary representation in Queensland, and faced ongoing court battles over electoral funding. The party was soundly defeated in 2001, polling just 4.35 % of the primary vote, with many of its former supporters returning to the coalition parties.

(Adapted from: http://www.australianpolitics.com/parties/ [19.05.2010])

Worksheet 10

Australia Quiz

1. **What is Australia's nickname?**
   a) Kiwi
   b) Aboriginal land
   c) Oz

2. **The continent of Australia is**
   a) a little larger than the USA.
   b) as large as the USA.
   c) a little smaller than the USA.

3. **Australia's population is approximately equal to**
   a) one third of that of Germany.
   b) a quarter of that of Germany.
   c) one fifth of that of Germany.

4. **Which of these is not the capital city of one of Australia's six states?**
   a) Darwin
   b) Adelaide
   c) Hobart

5. **Which of these animals does not appear on Australia's coat of arms?**
   a) emu
   b) kangaroo
   c) koala

6. **NYW is**
   a) a week of fun for yuppies interested in national culture.
   b) a new youth event celebrated throughout Australia.
   c) a national talent competition for young people.

7. **Which of these is a capital city?**
   a) Canberra
   b) Sydney
   c) Melbourne

8. **Which of the following was the first Aboriginal sportswoman to win an Olympic gold medal?**
   a) Samantha Stosur
   b) Cathy Freeman
   c) Libby Trickett

9. **Which of the following does not denote a musical instrument?**
   a) Yothu Yindi
   b) Yidaki
   c) Bilma

10. **Which song is Australia's official national anthem?**
    a) Waltzing Matilda
    b) Advance Australia Fair
    c) God Save the Queen (or King)

Worksheet 10

11. Which of these writers wrote "Finnikin of the Rock"?
a) Jane Harrison
b) Tim Winton
c) Melina Marchetta

12. Which grades are taught by the School of the Air in Central Australia?
a) pre-school only
b) from pre-school to year 7
c) from pre-school to year 9

13. The Royal Flying Doctor Service is provided free of charge
a) to people living and working in the Outback.
b) only to tourists.
c) to those who live, work and travel in Australia's Outback.

14. The first Aboriginal and Torres Strait Islander peoples arrived in Australia
a) about 40,000 to 80,000 years ago.
b) about 60,000 to 100,000 years ago.
c) more than 100,000 years ago.

15. The total amount of Aboriginal people living in Australia today is
a) about 260,000.
b) about 500,000.
c) about 1.1 million.

16. The Aboriginal sign  **means**
a) a place where the sun is always shining very brightly.
b) a waterhole people should avoid because of crocodiles living there.
c) a place where people are sitting around a fireplace.

17. Australia's national flower is
a) the sweet-smelling flowers of the eucalyptus tree.
b) the golden wattle.
c) the glorious red waratah.

18. The historic "sorry speech" was held by Prime Minister Kevin Rudd
a) in 2003.
b) in 2005.
c) in 2007.

19. In Australia, all citizens are required to enrol to vote at the age of
a) 16.
b) 18.
c) 21.

20. The Head of State of Australia is
a) the Queen (or King) of Great Britain.
b) the Governor-General.
c) the Prime Minister.

Worksheet 10 Solution

Australia Quiz

1. **What is Australia's nickname?**
   c) Oz

2. **The continent of Australia is**
   c) a little smaller than the USA.

3. **Australia's population is approximately equal to**
   b) a quarter of that of Germany.

4. **Which of these is not the capital city of one of Australia's six states?**
   a) Darwin

5. **Which of these animals does not appear on Australia's coat of arms?**
   c) koala

6. **NYW is**
   c) a national talent competition for young people.

7. **Which of these is a capital city?**
   a) Canberra
   b) Sydney
   c) Melbourne

8. **Which of the following was the first Aboriginal sportswoman to win an Olympic gold medal?**
   b) Cathy Freeman

9. **Which of the following does not denote a musical instrument?**
   a) Yothu Yindi

10. **Which song is Australia's official national anthem?**
    b) Advance Australia Fair

11. **Which of these writers wrote "Finnikin of the Rock"?**
    c) Melina Marchetta

12. **Which grades are taught by the School of the Air in Central Australia?**
    b) from pre-school to year 7

13. **The Royal Flying Doctor Service is provided free of charge**
    c) to those who live, work and travel in Australia's Outback.

14. **The first Aboriginal and Torres Strait Islander peoples arrived in Australia**
    a) about 40,000 to 80,000 years ago.

15. **The total amount of Aboriginal people living in Australia today is**
    b) about 500,000.

16. **The Aboriginal sign**  **means**
    c) a place where people are sitting around a fireplace.

17. **Australia's national flower is**
    b) the golden wattle.

18. **The historic "sorry speech" was held by Prime Minister Kevin Rudd**
    c) in 2007.

19. **In Australia, all citizens are required to enrol to vote at the age of**
    b) 18.

20. **The Head of State of Australia is**
    a) the Queen (or King) of Great Britain.

New Zealand – Getting started

Den Einstieg in das Thema „Neuseeland“ bilden wie bei Australien einige Fotografien aus dem Land, eine geografische Karte und das Erfassen des Vorwissens der Schüler. Die leichte Zuordnungsübung von Text zu Bild dient vor allem dazu, die Kursgruppe auf einige wesentliche Aspekte des Landes einzustimmen. Die sich dahinter verbergenden Themen werden im Laufe des Kurses wieder aufgegriffen.
Zum Wissen über das geografische Bild Neuseelands (Nordinsel, Südinsel und mehrere kleinere Inseln) gehört auch die Kenntnis der geografischen Lage des Inselstaats. Hierzu erfragt die Lehrkraft zunächst die Kenntnisse der Schüler bzw. bereitet das Thema in fächerübergreifender Kooperation mit der Lehrkraft für Geografie vor.
Eine Übersicht von Dokumentarfilmen über Land und Leute bietet die private Webseite von „Neuseelandhaus“: http://neuseeland.tv. Jeder Filmvorschlag enthält auch einen Link zu einer Videosequenz.

Solutions

Describe the pictures. Which beautiful regions and landscapes does New Zealand boast?

Activities p. 66

When describing the pictures, the students have to pay special attention to the use of the present progressive form of the verb to describe actions that are taking place in the picture (e. g. *sheep are running across the road*).
The photos show just a few of the different landscapes in New Zealand: rainforest in the North Island, high, snow-covered mountains and glaciers in the South Island; grassland areas in both islands; and the ocean surrounding New Zealand from all sides.

Which picture arouses your particular interest? Why?
Individual answers.

New Zealand – My First Encounter

Die Erstbegegnung mit Neuseeland bringt verschiedene Eindrücke mit sich: die exotische Kultur der Māori (die Menschen, ihre Körpertattoos, ihr künstlerisches und architektonisches Schaffen), die großartige Vielfalt von bezaubernden Landschaften auf relativ kleinem Gebiet, aber auch der besonders den Neuseeländern nachgesagte Ruf, einen ausgesprochenen Hang zu sportlicher Aktivität zu haben, oder die Tatsache, dass dieses kleine Land Heimstatt außerordentlich vieler Extremsportarten ist.
Da Sport das Thema eines der nächsten Kapitel ist, wird im ersten Kapitel – historisch gerecht – zunächst auf die Geschichte der einheimischen Bevölkerung des Landes eingegangen. Gelegentliche Querverbindungen zur Geschichte Australiens bieten sich dabei an. Im gesamten Kurs ist auch beim Thema „Neuseeland" eine fächerübergreifende Kooperation mit den Lehrkräften für Geschichte und Geografie denkbar.
Im Internet sind unzählige Seiten über Neuseeland zu finden. An Sachliteratur über dieses Land und Belletristik aus dem Land ist dagegen viel weniger zu finden als zum Beispiel über den großen Nachbarn Australien. Einen ersten authentischen Eindruck von Neuseeland können die Schüler im Netz beim Lesen der Schilderungen von jungen Menschen gewinnen, die in diesem Land studieren (www.newzealandeducated.com/int/en/stories).

I never knew this about New Zealand

Die in der gelben Infobox gegebenen Daten und Fakten bieten sich für weiterführende Gespräche und Recherchen an. Die einzelnen Absätze sollten deshalb nacheinander von der Klasse gelesen und sofort abgearbeitet werden. Die Fotos am Seitenrand illustrieren die wichtigsten Bedeutungen des Worts „kiwi/Kiwi".

Solutions

Activities p. 68

1. **Which meanings does the word 'kiwi' have?**
   Kiwi can denote a New Zealander, the endemic bird living only in New Zealand, a fruit (the kiwi fruit), and the New Zealand dollar.

2. **What do you know about New Zealand's population and languages?**
   New Zealand has a population of about 4.3 million people (July 2009). Three languages have an official status: in addition to English and Māori, the sign language of the deaf community in New Zealand became official in April 2006.

3. **Make a fact sheet of what you already know about Aotearoa. Keep this record until you have finished the New Zealand course. Later, you can compare your knowledge about the 'long white cloud' before and after you have completed this course.**
   Individual answers.
   At the end of the course, it will be a great surprise for the students to see how much they have learned about this country.

4. **Search the web for discoverers and founders of New Zealand. Find out what they are famous for and give a talk about each of them: Abel Tasman, James Cook, Edward Gibbon Wakefield, William Hobson.**

Abel Tasman (1603–1659): Dutch seafarer, explorer, and merchant; his crew was the first known European expedition to reach the islands of Van Diemen's Land (now Tasmania) and New Zealand; in 1643, he landed on the coast of New Zealand; in his journal, Tasman called this land "groot hooch verheven landt" (a large land, lifted up high) and named it "Staten Landt", which refers to the "Land of the (Dutch) States-General".
James Cook (1728–1779): British explorer, navigator and cartographer; he was the first European to have contact with the eastern coastline of Australia, exploring around the Great Barrier Reef in 1770; on 6th October 1769, Cook landed on the east coast of New Zealand with his ship "The Endeavour", and two days later sailed into a bay and set anchor at the entrance of a small river in Tuuranga-nui (today's Poverty Bay, near modern city of Gisborne); Cook named a peninsula in this bay "Young Nick's Head" after Nicholas Young who had first sighted land.
Edward Gibbon Wakefield (1796–1862): E. G. Wakefield was a British politician who was a leading figure in the early colonization of South Australia and New Zealand; he was also an influential member of the New Zealand Association which, in the colonization of this country, saw an important tool for social engineering; in 1837, the Colonial Office gave the New Zealand Association a charter to promote settlement in New Zealand.
William Hobson (1792–1842): Captain Hobson, born in Ireland, was the first Governor of New Zealand and co-author of the Treaty of Waitangi; Hobson arrived in the Bay of Islands on 29th January, 1840 (which is now celebrated on the North Island as Auckland Anniversary Day) with a small group of officials; together with Willoughby Shortland, Francis Fisher and three Justices of the Peace, he belonged to the Legislative Council of New Zealand (which constituted the then government).

The Legend of Māui

Die Schöpfungsgeschichte ist in der Mythologie der Māori eng mit der Gestalt der den Staat bildenden beiden großen Inseln verbunden. Bei der Lektüre sollte deshalb die Karte Neuseelands möglichst zur Hand sein.

Haere Mai! – Te Reo Māori

Heute wird Māori nur noch von wenig mehr als 150 000 Menschen gesprochen. Dieses Idiom zählt deshalb zu den Minderheitensprachen so wie Sorbisch oder Friesisch in Deutschland bzw. Walisisch in Großbritannien. Um diese Besonderheit zu verdeutlichen, wird den Schülern mit Aufgabe 2 ein darauf bezogener Auftrag erteilt.
Māori ist eine polynesische Sprache und relativ einfach. Sie kennt nur fünf Vokale und zehn Konsonanten, deren Aussprache dem Schriftbild in der Regel sehr nahe kommt. In diesem Kurs werden die Schüler eine Reihe von Māoriwörtern kennenlernen und angehalten werden, sich weiter mit der Sprache zu beschäftigen.

Solutions

1. **Look at the map of New Zealand and try to make out the tail and the mouth of the fish. Try retelling the Māori legend in your own words.** Activities p. 69

When retelling the legend, the students might want to show the places they are speaking about on the map. For this reason, a map of New Zealand should be at hand.

2. **Compare the history of the Māori language to the fate of minority languages such as Welsh in the UK, or Friesian or Sorbian in Germany.**
It can be interesting for the class to learn more about each of these minority languages and compare them to Māori. This can be done either in the form of short talks given to the class or in a summarizing grid like the one shown below.

Māori	Māori is an Eastern Polynesian language that is regarded as endangered because it is spoken by only 150,000 people; the language is closely related to the Cook Islands Māori and Tahitian. In 1987, Māori became one of three official languages in New Zealand so many place names and official institutions have both an English and a Māori name. Since March 2004, Māori Television has been broadcasting, partly in Māori, and in 2008, a second channel broadcasting entirely in this language was launched. Since 1975, a government-funded Māori Language Week has been celebrated every year to further support the minority language.
Welsh	About 500,000 people in Wales can speak, read and write Welsh, a Celtic language; however, there are many more speakers of this language around the world. In some regions of Wales, Welsh is the first language in schools and is widely spoken in households and public institutions. In 1977, the Welsh-language radio station BBC Radio Cymru was established, followed by the Welsh language TV channel S4C in 1982.
Sorbian	Sorbian is a Slavic language spoken by about 50,000 people in a region called Lusatia that is located in former East Germany approximately between Lubben in the north and Budysin (Bautzen) in the south. The cultural centre of the Sorbs, the Domowina Institution, is in Budysin, where a theatre presents plays in Sorbian; newspapers and books are also published in this language, and at many schools, Sorbian is taught as a foreign language.
Friesian	The Friesians are a Germanic people living in parts of The Netherlands and in North Germany along the coast of the North Sea. Altogether, there are three varieties of the Friesian language: North, West and Saterland Friesian spoken by a total of about 500,000 people of the different Friesian ethnic groups; Saterland and North Frisian are officially recognised as minority languages in Germany.

Treaty of Waitangi

Das wichtigste Dokument in Neuseelands Geschichte der Neuzeit ist der „Vertrag von Waitangi". Er findet überall in Neuseeland ausdrückliche Würdigung, insbesondere natürlich in Waitangi, dem Ort im äußersten Norden Neuseelands, wo der Vertrag 1840 abgeschlossen wurde. Ein Besuch des Museumskomplexes mit dem prächtigen Māorihaus (*marae*) lohnt sich, selbst wenn sich die Schüler auch vorerst nur einige Bilder im Internet ansehen können.
Eine sehr ausführliche Darstellung aller Ereignisse und einen Zugang zu den Dokumenten finden die Schüler auf der Webseite www.nzhistory.net.nz.
Zum englischen Vertragstext werden im Internet einige Erklärungen gegeben, die sein Verständnis erleichtern. Sie werden hier im Lehrerbuch abgedruckt, damit die Lehrkraft sie für die Schüler kopieren und die Informationen in das Unterrichtsgespräch über den Vertrag einfließen lassen kann (s. **Worksheet 11** und **Worksheet 12**). Die Arbeitsblätter können nach dem Ermessen der Lehrkraft an verschiedenen didaktischen Orten

eingesetzt und den Schülern entweder als Folien- oder Papierkopie zugänglich gemacht werden.
Abbildungen der Handschriften von William Hobson zum Treaty of Waitangi finden sich unter www.celticnz.org/TreatyBook/Chapter05a.htm.
Das Schriftdokument des *Treaty of Waitangi* ist im Internet in Englisch und Māori zu finden. Ein zumindest oberflächlicher Vergleich ist interessant. In dem auf Seite 70 (SB) abgedruckten Dokument sind die Zwischenüberschriften bereits in Māori belassen worden, um den Schülern die Gelegenheit zu geben zu erraten, was diese bedeuten könnten.
Die Māori-Fassung des Vertrags (**Worksheet 13**) kann der Klasse fakultativ als Folie gezeigt werden, um sie mit der fremden Sprache auch visuell etwas näher bekannt zu machen.

Parihaka – A Symbol of Protest

Nach der Unterzeichnung des Vertrags von Waitangi waren durchaus nicht alle Stämme der Māori mit der Unterwerfung unter die britische Oberherrschaft einverstanden. Vor allem im stärker besiedelten Norden wehrten sich einige von ihnen energisch.
Der Text „Parihaka – A Symbol of Protest" liest sich für die Schüler wie vergleichbare andere Beschreibungen von Volksaufständen. Bei der Besprechung des Textes können deshalb auch Vergleiche gezogen werden mit ähnlichen politischen Auseinandersetzungen, nicht zuletzt mit der „friedlichen Revolution" in der DDR 1989.

Solutions

Activities p. 71

1. **Who were Te Whiti o Rongomai and Tohu Kakahi and what did they fight against and what for?**
   Te Whiti o Rongomai and Tohu Kakahi both of Te Atiawa and Taranaki in the North Island, were pacifists and Māori spiritual leaders, who ignored the fact that their land had been officially confiscated by the British conquerors. They wanted to continue living in their own way. Since they had not signed the Treaty of Waitangi, they strongly insisted that the Treaty and the confiscation of their land were illegal. For this reason, they fought the British settlers, especially the surveyors who wanted to mark out land for settlement.

2. **Was the Māori's fight successful in the end? Try to give a first answer to this question. However, keep this question in mind. You will be able to answer it more definitely when you have finished this book.**
   As we know today, the Māori's fight was not successful. The British settlers came and stayed in New Zealand and made it a prospering Western-style country.
   Further reading will show, however, that the Māori today play an important role in their country, which can, for example, be seen from the fact that their language is one of the official languages in New Zealand.

3. **Give a speech on the Treaty of Waitangi and the Parihaka movement. Explain why they are of particular importance to New Zealand.**
   Individual answers. The speech should not exceed 10–15 minutes so that the class (and the teacher) have the chance to ask some questions, and the speaker the time to answer them. In their talk, the students should show that the Treaty of Waitangi and the Māori Parihaka movement have laid the foundations for the cultural and political strength of the Māori in New Zealand's society (also see the chapter "Māori Culture in New Zealand and Abroad").

Worksheet 11

The Treaty of Waitangi

The following translation of the Māori text of the Treaty was done by former Tribunal member Professor Sir Hugh Kawharu.

Victoria, the Queen of England, in her concern to protect the chiefs and the subtribes of New Zealand and in her desire to preserve their chieftainship[1] and their lands to them and to maintain peace[2] and good order considers it just to appoint an administrator[3] one who will negotiate with the people of New Zealand to the end that their chiefs will agree to the Queen's Government being established over all parts of this land and (adjoining) islands[4] and also because there are many of her subjects already living on this land and others yet to come. So the Queen desires to establish a government so that no evil will come to Māori and European living in a state of lawlessness. So the Queen has appointed me, William Hobson, a Captain in the Royal Navy to be Governor for all parts of New Zealand (both those) shortly to be received by the Queen and (those) to be received hereafter and presents[5] to the chiefs of the Confederation chiefs of the subtribes of New Zealand and other chiefs these laws set out here.

The first

The Chiefs of the Confederation and all the Chiefs who have not joined that Confederation give absolutely to the Queen of England for ever the complete government[6] over their land.

The second

The Queen of England agrees to protect the chiefs, the subtribes and all the people of New Zealand in the unqualified exercise[7] of their chieftainship over their lands, villages and all their treasures[8]. But on the other hand the Chiefs of the Confederation and all the Chiefs will sell[9] land to the Queen at a price agreed to by the person owning it and by the person buying it (the latter being) appointed by the Queen as her purchase agent.

The third

For this agreed arrangement therefore concerning the Government of the Queen, the Queen of England will protect all the ordinary people of New Zealand and will give them the same rights and duties[10] of citizenship as the people of England[11].

(Source: www.waitangi-tribunal.govt.nz/treaty/kawharutranslation.asp [19.05.2010])

Worksheet 12

Footnotes to the Treaty of Waitangi

---

1 "chieftainship": This concept has to be understood in the context of Māori social and political organization as it stood in 1840. The accepted approximation today is "trusteeship".
2 "Peace": Māori *rongo*, seemingly a missionary usage (*rongo* – to hear, i.e. hear the "Word" – the "message" of peace and goodwill, etc.).
3 Literally "Chief" (*Rangatira*) here is, of course, ambiguous. Clearly, a European could not be a Māori, but the word could well have implied a trustee-like role rather than that of a mere "functionary". Māori speeches at Waitangi in 1840 refer to Hobson being or becoming a "father" for the Māori people. Certainly, this attitude has been held towards the person of the Crown down to the present day – hence the continued expectations and commitments entailed in the Treaty.
4 "Islands" i.e. coastal, not of the Pacific.
5 Literally "making", i.e. "offering" or "saying" – but not "inviting to concur".
6 "Government": *kawanatanga*. There could be no possibility of the Māori signatories having any understanding of government in the sense of "sovereignty", i.e. any understanding on the basis of experience or cultural precedent.
7 "Unqualified exercise" of the chieftainship would emphasise to a chief the Queen's intention to give them complete control according to their customs. *Tino* has the connotation of "quintessential".
8 "Treasures": *taonga*. As submissions to the Waitangi Tribunal concerning the Māori language have made clear, *"taonga"* refers to all dimensions of a tribal group's estate – material and non-material –, heirlooms and *wahi tapu* (sacred places), ancestral lore and *whakapapa* (genealogies), etc.
9 Māori *hokonga*, literally "sale and purchase". *Hoko* means to buy or sell.
10 "Rights and duties": Māori at Waitangi in 1840 refer to Hobson being or becoming a "father" for the Māori people. Certainly, this attitude has been held towards the person of the Crown down to the present day – hence the continued expectations and commitments entailed in the Treaty.
11 There is, however, a more profound problem about *tikanga*. There is a real sense here of the Queen "protecting" (i.e. allowing the preservation of) the Māori people's *tikanga* (i.e. customs) since no Māori could have had any understanding whatever of British *tikanga* (i.e. the rights and duties of British subjects). This, then, reinforces the guarantees in Article 2.

(from: www.postcolonialweb.org/nz/dewes3.html [19.05.2010])

Worksheet 13

Tiriti o Waitangi

Ko Wikitoria te Kuini o Ingarani i tana mahara atawai ki nga Rangatira me nga Hapu o Nu Tirani i tana hiahia hoki kia tohungia ki a ratou o ratou rangatiratanga me to ratou wenua, a kia mau tonu hoki te Rongo ki a ratou me te Atanoho hoki kua wakaaro ia he mea tika kia tukua mai tetahi Rangatira – hei kai wakarite ki nga Tangata Māori o Nu Tirani – kia wakaaetia e nga Rangatira Māori te Kawanatanga o te Kuini ki nga wahikatoa o te Wenua nei me nga Motu – na te mea hoki he tokomaha ke nga tangata o tona Iwi Kua noho ki tenei wenua, a e haere mai nei.
Na ko te Kuini e hiahia ana kia wakaritea te Kawanatanga kia kaua ai nga kino e puta mai ki te tangata Māori ki te Pakeha e noho ture kore ana.
Na, kua pai te Kuini kia tukua a hau a Wiremu Hopihona he Kapitana i te Roiara Nawi hei Kawana mo nga wahi katoa o Nu Tirani e tukua aianei, amoa atu ki te Kuini, e mea atu ana ia ki nga Rangatira o te wakaminenga o nga hapu o Nu Tirani me era Rangatira atu enei ture ka korerotia nei.

KO TE TUATAHI

Ko nga Rangatira o te wakaminenga me nga Rangatira katoa hoki ki hai i uru ki taua wakaminenga ka tuku rawa atu ki te Kuini o Ingarani ake tonu atu – te Kawanatanga katoa o ratou wenua.

KO TE TUARUA

Ko te Kuini o Ingarani ka wakarite ka wakaae ki nga Rangatira ki nga hapu – ki nga tangata katoa o Nu Tirani te tino rangatiratanga o ratou wenua o ratou kainga me o ratou taonga katoa. Otiia ko nga Rangatira o te wakaminenga me nga Rangatira katoa atu ka tuku ki te Kuini te hokonga o era wahi wenua e pai ai te tangata nona te Wenua – ki te ritenga o te utu e wakaritea ai e ratou ko te kai hoko e meatia nei e te Kuini hei kai hoko mona.

KO TE TUATORU

Hei wakaritenga mai hoki tenei mo te wakaaetanga ki te Kawanatanga o te Kuini – Ka tiakina e te Kuini o Ingarani nga tangata Māori katoa o Nu Tirani ka tukua ki a ratou nga tikanga katoa rite tahi ki ana mea ki nga tangata o Ingarani.

[signed] William Hobson Consul & Lieutenant Governor

Na ko matou ko nga Rangatira o te Wakaminenga o nga hapu o Nu Tirani ka huihui nei ki Waitangi ko matou hoki ko nga Rangatira o Nu Tirani ka kite nei i te ritenga o enei kupu, ka tangohia ka wakaaetia katoatia e matou, koia ka tohungia ai o matou ingoa o matou tohu.
Ka meatia tenei ki Waitangi i te ono o nga ra o Pepueri i te tau kotahi mano, e waru rau e wa te kau o to tatou Ariki.

(Source: http://goaustralia.about.com/od/discovernewzealand/a/treaty2.htm [19.05.2010])

Māori Then and Today

Dieses Kapitel ist ganz der Rolle der Māori in der heutigen Gesellschaft gewidmet und wirft ein Streiflicht auf ihre jüngste Geschichte.
Dieses Thema ist dazu geeignet, dass sich die Schüler über die vorhandenen Texte und Bilder hinaus mit der Māorikultur und ihrer Bedeutung für das heutige Neuseeland auseinandersetzen. Vielleicht nehmen sie sogar Kontakt zu einer Schule auf (s. auch das nächste Kapitel). Die Ergebnisse dieser Beschäftigung können auf vielfältige Weise veröffentlicht werden.

I never knew this about New Zealand

In der gelben Infobox lernen die Schüler außer einer ganzen Reihe von Fakten und Daten auch wieder einige Māoriwörter kennen, die in den Wortschatz des neuseeländischen Englisch übernommen wurden: *Pākeha* (die weißen europäischen Neuseeländer), *kohanga reo* („Sprachnester", womit eine Einrichtung für Vorschulkinder der Māori gemeint ist, in denen sie die Sprache ihrer Vorfahren lernen können), *haka* (ein ritualer Begrüßungs- und Kampftanz der Māori), und *marae* (das schön geschmückte Versammlungshaus der Māoristämme). Spätestens an dieser Stelle kann die Lehrkraft die Schüler auffordern, sich (fakultativ?) eine Liste von Māoriwörtern anzulegen.
Der auf der Seite 72 abgedruckte Ortsname ist interessant und lustig zu lesen. Er dient zur Belebung des Unterrichts und eventuell zum Üben des Lesens von Māoriwörtern. Einen nachhaltigen Eindruck bei den Schülern hinterlässt es erfahrungsgemäß, wenn die Lehrkraft dieses lange Wort auswendig vortragen kann, was sehr zur Motivation für den Englischunterricht beizutragen vermag.

Māori Ethnic Population – Te Momo Iwi Māori

Obwohl die absolute Zahl der Māori (nicht einmal 600,000) relativ gering ist, ist ihr prozentualer Anteil an der Bevölkerung immerhin wesentlich größer als der der *Indigenous people* an der Bevölkerung Australiens. Der unter diesem Text eingefügte Bevölkerungsbaum fordert geradezu heraus, seine Form mit dem Deutschlands zu vergleichen. Nach der Lektüre des Textes sowie der ausführlichen Beschreibung und Interpretation des Bevölkerungsbaums sollte die Lehrkraft deshalb das Gespräch auf den Vergleich mit Deutschland oder auch auf den Vergleich mit Minderheiten in anderen Ländern bringen.

Solutions

Activities p. 73

1. **Read the text on page 68/69 about the development of the Māori identity and analyse the bar chart on this page. Organise the numbers from the text in the form of two pie charts, then prepare a talk in which you interpret the numbers given in your charts. In your talk, answer this question: How has the Māori identity developed in recent years?**
   See the examples on **Worksheet 14**.

The numbers clearly show that the Māori ethnic population in New Zealand has been growing in recent years. For example, it grew from 434,847 in 1991 to 565,329 in 2006. This has resulted from the Government's supportive policies as well as of the Māori's positive role in New Zealand's society.
There were 3,516,000 people in New Zealand in 1991 (source: http://en.wikipedia.org/wiki/1991_in_New_Zealand), and 4,143,279 people in 2006 (www.northshorecity.govt.nz). These figures form the basis for the percentages used in the pie charts on **Worksheet 14**. In addition to these first two pie charts, the worksheet also shows a pie chart illustrating the ethnicity distribution within the Māori population.

2. **Compare the bar chart of the Māori population with the age distribution of the population of Germany. Which differences do you notice? What might be the reasons for these differences? Discuss.**
The population tree of Germany is shown on **Worksheet 15**. If the students do not have access to a computer in school or at home, the teacher may show them this graph. As can be seen, most of the people in Germany are 40 to 50 years old, whereas New Zealand's population is dominated by children and young people up to 20 years of age. This means that, in ten years, Germany will have a very big share of 50 to 60-year-olds. This is what we call the aging of Germany's population.
There are various reasons for these differences. The main reasons are:
   - people in Germany tend to live longer because of the excellent health care in our country,
   - the massive decline in the birth rate since 1990. As shown above, the latter has not been seen in New Zealand.

3. **Listen to New Zealand's national anthem and analyse its message: http://folksong.org.nz/e_ihowa_atua.**
On the website www.maorilanguage.net, the students can listen to the national anthem of New Zealand and learn other songs of this country.

National Anthem of New Zealand

God of Nations at thy feet
In the bonds of love we meet;
Hear our voices we entreat;
God defend our free land;
Guard Pacific's triple star;
From the shafts of strife and war;
Make her praises heard afar
God defend New Zealand.

E Ihoā Atua,
O ngā iwi mātou rā;
Āta whakarongona,
Me aroha noa;
Kia hua ko te pai
Kia tau to ata whai;
Manaakitia mai
Aotearoa

The anthem describes New Zealand (*Aotearoa*) as a land of the Lord in which people of different ethnicities can live together in freedom, peace and love and pray to God to protect their country from discord and war.

Māori Culture in New Zealand and Abroad

In fünf Zeitungsausschnitten wird die Rolle deutlich, die die Māori heute in der neuseeländischen Gesellschaft spielen. Jeder Beitrag wird durch eine passende Illustration ergänzt.
Die Lektüre der Artikel sollte möglichst in der im Alltag üblichen Weise erfolgen, nämlich zunächst als kursives Lesen und erst später als aufsuchendes Lesen, wenn bestimmte Themen weiter verfolgt werden sollen.

Solutions

Activities p. 75

1. **How does the first text explain the term *Manaakitanga*?**
The Māori word *manaakitanga* describes the deeply-rooted tradition of hospitality in Māori culture. It includes guardianship (*whenua*) and treasuring (*taaonga*), native people (*tangata*), and visitors (*manuhiri*). *Manaakitanga* is always practised when visitors or guests first arrive.

2. **Sum up in one-sentence statements what each of the five articles deals with. Begin your summaries like this: "The text '(title)' is about ..."**
1) The article "Feel the spirit – Manaakitanga" explains what the Māori welcome ceremony *Manaakitanga* is about.
2) In the text "Leaders get experience", the Dominion Post reports about the *tuakana* art leadership programme at Auckland University, which gives talented Māori and Pasifika students studying Arts academic support over a one year period as well as future internship opportunities.
3) The text "tamariki on tv" reports about the Kohanga Reo o Ranana group in London, which runs workshops for Māori children "to ensure they know about their heritage even though they are growing up so far away from home".
4) The article "Kiwis one short in medal hunt – Paralympics" is about the 2008 Paralympics in Beijing where powerlifter George Taamaru of Auckland unfortunately failed to win a medal.
5) The fifth article "Māori heritage in Great Britain" tells the reader about an ancient Māori flagpole that was brought to the Museum of Archaeology and Anthropology in Cambridge, UK in 1920.

3. **What is the frequent use of Māori words in everyday life a sign of?**
Māori words are often used in New Zealand English, both orally and in written form. This shows that the Māori culture today plays a dominant role in New Zealand's society.

4. **Surf the web for more information about these Māori terms that are frequently used in New Zealand English: marae, haka, hongi, moko, pouhaki. Make a poster which explains and illustrates them.**
marae: The marae is either a sacred open meeting area or the communal meeting house on it.
haka: The haka is a traditional form of dance of the Māori that is performed by a group.
hongi: The hongi is the traditional Māori form of greeting by pressing one's nose and forehead to another person, this way exchanging their 'breath of life' or spirit.
moko: The moko is the traditional tattoo of the Māori.
pouhaki: Pouhaki is the Māori name for the traditional carved flagpoles erected as a sign of sovereignty.

The pictures in **Worksheet 16** illustrate these words. The students might, however, find different pictures and illustrations on the Internet or in books. For more information about the Māori language see http://maorilanguage.info.

Captions and sources:

A. Marae-like dwelling house in Rotorua – private photo, Kathrin Becker
B. Rugby team practising the haka before the match begins – private photo, Kathrin Becker
C. New Zealand Prime Minister John Key (right) receives a hongi from Professor Whatarangi Winiata, President of the Māori Party; www.zimbio.com
D. Face moko – Rotorua Visitor Guide
E. Pouhaki in front of the Wainuiomata Marae – www.wainuiomatamarae.org.nz/pouhaki.JPG

5. If you want to know more about Māori life and culture, visit NZ's National Museum 'Te Papa': www.tepapa.govt.nz. Write a letter in which you give reasons why it is worth visiting.

Individual answers. The letter should keep to the normal format for this sort of text and not only include information about the "Te Papa" but also some personal elements such as the correct beginning and ending of letters.

Worksheet 14

Development of the Māori Population in New Zealand

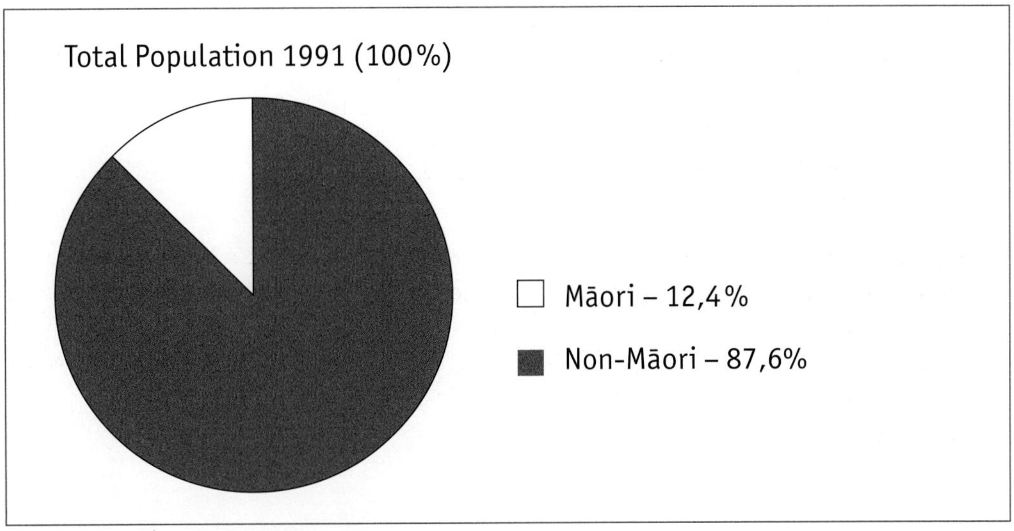

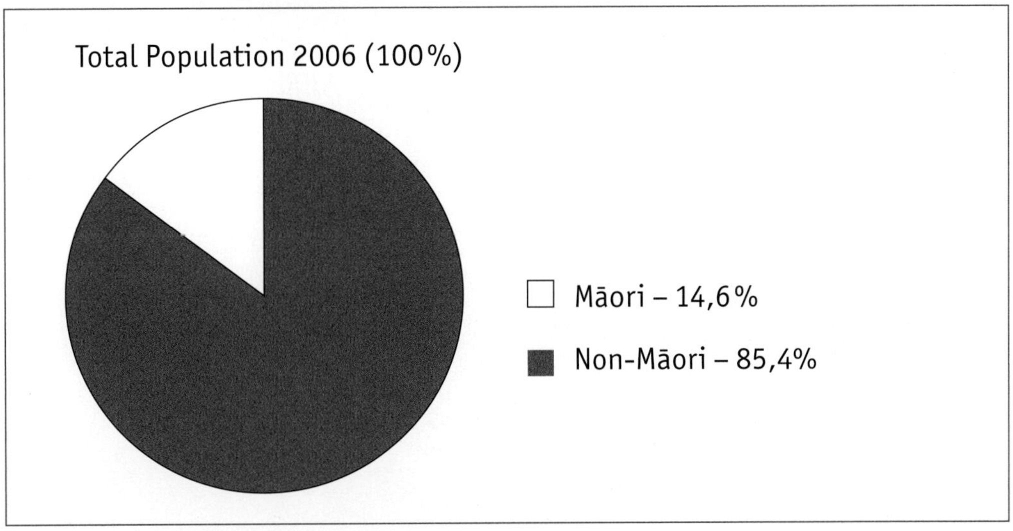

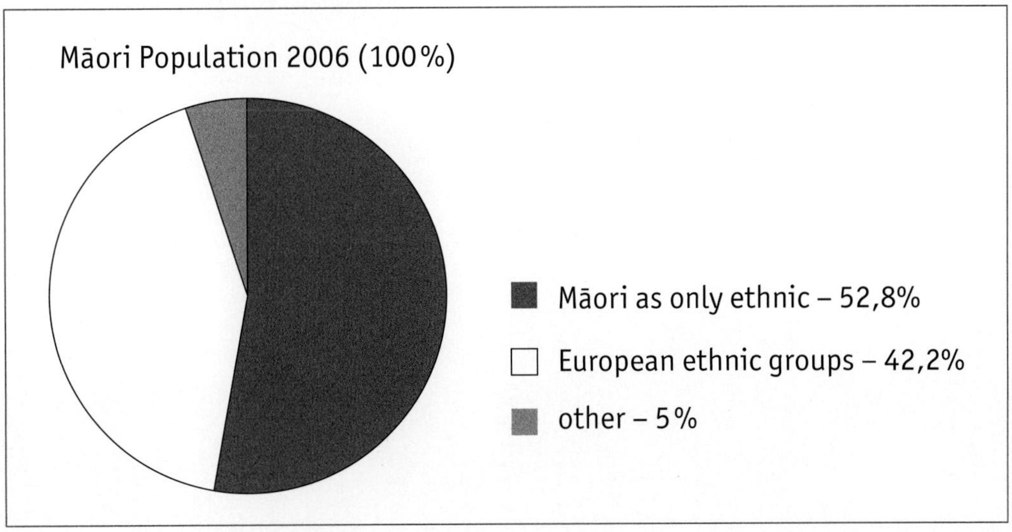

Worksheet 15

Population Tree of Germany in 2009

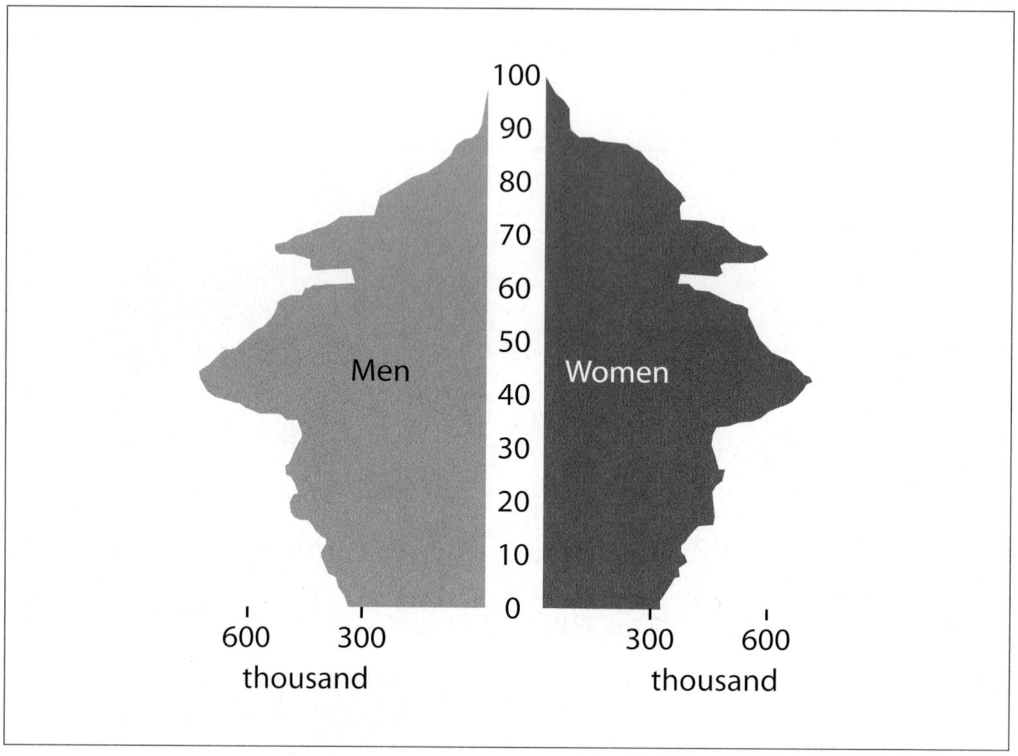

Worksheet 16

Māori Words in Illustrations

A

B

E

A: Marae, B: Haka, C: Hongi,
D: Moko, E: Pouhaki

C

D

A High School Year in Aoteroa

In Neuseeland absolvieren nicht wenige Schüler und Studenten einen Teil ihrer Schulzeit bzw. ihres Studiums. Der hier abgedruckte anonymisierte Brief wurde von einer deutschen Schülerin geschrieben. Er kann die Schüler der Kursstufe veranlassen, das Schulsystem des Landes näher zu betrachten (wenn auch ein Jahr an einer High School nicht mehr für sie in Frage kommt) und sich für Studienmöglichkeiten an einer der acht staatlichen oder einer der ungleich teureren privaten Universitäten Neuseelands zu interessieren.
Vor der Entscheidung für ein Studienjahr oder Semester in Neuseeland oder Australien kann auch ein privater Test stehen, wie gut die Englischkenntnisse sind. Sehr gut geeignet dafür ist die Webseite www.testden.com/scripts/aspect/intro.asp. Sie lässt sich auch im Unterricht einsetzen.
Die mannigfachen Informationen über Schulen in Neuseeland kann die Lehrkraft nutzen, um sie die Schüler mit ihrer eigenen Schule vergleichen zu lassen bzw. Ideen zu entwickeln, wie sie sich eine gute Schule vorstellen. In diesem Sinn kann der Unterrichtsstoff an dieser Stelle weit über das landeskundliche Thema hinausgehen.

New Plymouth Girls' High School

In diesem Buch können nur einige wenige Daten über die Schule der Briefschreiberin vermittelt und wenige Bilder gezeigt werden. Ausführlichere Angaben über diese Mädchenschule finden sich auf der Webseite www.npghs.com und über viele andere Schulen unter www.minedu.govt.nz/theMinistry/EducationInNewZealand.aspx.
Das Bild auf Seite 69 und das unterste Bild auf Seite 77 zeigen Mädchen der Schule bei der Ausführung eines *haka* in der traditionellen Kleidung. Die Röcke bestehen aus vielen kürzeren „Röhrchen“ (auf Māori *piupiu*) aus natürlichem Material oder Plaste, die an einem Gürtel befestigt sind.

Rotorua Boys' High School

Während die Mädchenschule an der nördlichen Westküste liegt, befindet sich diese *High School* für Jungen im Zentrum der Nordinsel, in Rotorua, das auch ein Touristenzentrum ist. Besonders interessant am Text über die *Boys' High School* in Rotorua sind die umfänglich beschriebenen Werte, die die Schüler dieser Einrichtung mitbringen bzw. erwerben sollen. Es bietet sich an, die Aufzählung der fünf genannten Werte mit Wertvorstellungen deutscher Schüler zu vergleichen:

Pūmau – being strong of character,
Whakaatu ngārahutanga – demonstrating leadership,
Ūpoko pakaru – showing commitment,
Kapo huanga – taking opportunities (den Schülern wird in der Diskussion dazu wahrscheinlich die Redensart „seize the day“ oder „carpe diem“ einfallen),
Hiratanga – striving for excellence.

Solutions

Activities p. 79

1. **A friend of yours wants to know what school life is like in New Zealand. Sum up in German what you have learned from the texts.**
This is an opportunity to practise mediation. The teacher could also ask one of the students to tell the others about school in New Zealand in English, and another one to mediate, i. e. not to translate word by word but to sum up the main facts in German.
Example:
Das Schuljahr beginnt und endet zu anderen Zeiten als in Deutschland. In Klasse 12 müssen die Schüler hier nur fünf Fächer wählen, aber es gibt eine viel größere Auswahl als normalerweise in Deutschland.
Jeden Morgen findet eine Klassenstunde statt, in der darüber gesprochen wird, was in der Schule los ist oder was die Klasse demnächst zu tun hat. Ungefähr zweimal in der Woche kommt in der Klassenstunde die ganze Schule zusammen und wird durch die Schulleitung instruiert über die anstehenden Vorhaben.
Die Schule, über die die deutsche Schülerin schreibt, ist riesig, sie hat etwa 1500 Schüler – und alle sind Mädchen! Es gibt aber auch Schulen nur für Jungen.
In Neuseeland müssen die Schüler Schuluniformen tragen, deren Farbe und Form vorgeschrieben sind.
In den Schulprospekten werden ganz genau die Ziele der Schule umrissen: gute Arbeits- und Lernbedingungen für alle zu schaffen, die Schüler zu ermutigen, ihr Bestes zu geben, ihnen umfassende Möglichkeiten für sportliche, kulturelle und soziale Aktivitäten anzubieten und auch über die Schule hinaus zu denken und zu handeln.
Die Lernprinzipien und die allgemeinen Werte der High Schools sind fest umrissen. Zu den grundlegenden Prinzipien gehört es, akademische und sportliche Höchstleistungen zu erzielen, sich kulturell zu betätigen, sich Führungsqualitäten anzueignen und sich zu einem vollwertigen Bürger zu entwickeln.
Manche Schulen haben Internate wie in Deutschland.
Ausländische Schüler sind in den Schulen gern gesehen. Es gibt für sie auch individuelle Programme.
NB: Dem Text im Schülerbuch ist nicht zu entnehmen, dass es in Neuseeland auch koedukative Schulversuche gibt.

2. **After you have read about the educational and social aims of NPGHS and RBHS, discuss what the principles and aims of your school are or should be. Work in groups to write different statements on this topic.**
After discussing and writing down their ideas for possible principles and aims of their own school, the students can present the results of their brainstorming to the class, or the teacher can organise a class discussion.

3. **Choose one topic to write an essay about:**
a) Are co-educational schools better than boys- or girls-only schools?
b) The pros and cons of wearing school uniforms.
c) Ad astra per aspera – a motto for our school.
The essay can be written at home or in class and graded by the teacher.

4. **Surf the Internet to collect more information about both schools. Imagine you want to enrol in one of them. Write a formal letter of application in which you give reasons why you want to attend this school.**
Writing letters of application (whether in German or English) is an important skill for the students to have. Therefore, the teacher should make sure that the students know how to write such a letter. To this end, the teacher might want to use the article "Applying for a job" in *Praxis Englisch* (August 2009, pp. 42 to 45), which includes writing a CV.

Neuseeland ist nicht von ungefähr Ursprungsland mehrerer Extremsportarten und hat unter anderem das Bungeespringen als Nervenkitzel populär gemacht. Den Neuseeländern wird nachgesagt, dass sie sportlich besonders aktiv sind. Das gilt ganz besonders natürlich für alle Wassersportarten auf dem Meer, aber auch zum Beispiel für das *white water rafting*.
Da dieses Thema für die Schüler sicherlich von besonderem Interesse ist, sollte die Lehrkraft Anregungen der Klasse möglichst aufgreifen und z. B. einige Sportarten im Unterricht oder in Postern vorstellen lassen.

New Zealanders Are People of Action

In diesem Text gewinnen die Schüler einen Überblick über die verschiedenen Freizeit- und Leistungssportaktivitäten der Neuseeländer. Schon hier können sie beginnen, sich eine Übersicht über die wichtigsten in Neuseeland betriebenen Sportarten zu verschaffen.
Die Fotos am Bildrand dieser Seite dokumentieren eine Wildwasserfahrt, die für „Kiwis" wie für Touristen gleichermaßen aufregend ist.
Besonders interessant wird möglicherweise die statistische Darstellung in der Tabelle „Top five sports played by young people" sein, denn erstens rangieren ganz andere Sportarten an oberster Stelle als in Deutschland, und zweitens ist im Vergleich von Sportverbänden (links) und aktiver Freizeitbeschäftigung (rechts) eine deutlich unterschiedliche Gewichtung des Interesses an den verschiedenen Disziplinen zu erkennen. Die Tabelle sollte von der Klasse zunächst still gelesen und dann in ganzen Sätzen vorgetragen und zum Schluss interpretiert werden.
Umfassende Informationen über die beliebtesten Sportarten Jugendlicher und Erwachsener in Neuseeland bietet die Webseite: www.sparc.org.nz. Einige neuseeländische Sportler werden die Schüler vielleicht auch kennen, wie zum Beispiel die Kugelstoßerin Valerie Vili, Olympiasiegerin von Peking 2008 und Weltmeisterin in Berlin 2009.

Bungee Jumping

Bevor die zusammenfassenden Aufgaben für beide Seiten über Sport in Neuseeland erteilt werden, lesen die Schüler etwas über die Geschichte des *bungee jumping* sowie kurze Zitate aus den Blogs von jungen Menschen, die zum ersten Mal den Sprung in die Tiefe gewagt haben. Nützlich ist es auch, in ein Bungee-Jumping-Forum hineinzusehen und sich dort Fakten und Anregungen zu holen.
Blogs werden nicht in Standardsprache geschrieben. Die Schüler werden aber keine Probleme mit der Kleinschreibung am Satzanfang oder umgangssprachlichen Ausdrücken (wanna, what a rush) oder dem im Netz stehenden, hier aber ausgelassenen *four-letter-word* haben.

Solutions

Activities p. 81

1. **After reading the table on page 80, compare which sports are practised in NZ schools and in your school or area. Is there a sport you would like to be able to do in your school or community? Why?**
The main aim of this exercise is to have the students speak with each other and with the teacher. The comparison can, however, also be presented in written form.

2. **According to the New Zealand Herald, rugby, cricket, league, soccer, netball, basketball, golf, tennis, motorsport, yachting and racing are among the most popular of New Zealand's sports. Search the web for current information on these disciplines in Aotearoa: www.nzherald.co.nz/sport/news/headlines.cfm?c_id=4.**
Individual answers. The favourite sport of most New Zealanders is rugby, and their favourite team – the All Blacks.
"According to the New York Times, golf and rugby appear the favorites to be the sports added to the 2016 Summer Olympics ..." (from: www.olympic-rugby.org, 12 August 2009)

3. **Find out and explain what these extreme sports are about: mountain biking, white water rafting, bungee jumping, barefoot skiing, base jumping, kite landboarding, jetboating, skydiving.**
mountain biking: Mountain biking is the sport of riding bicycles off-road, often over rough terrain, using specially-equipped mountain bikes or hybrid road bikes.
white water rafting: White water rafting or simply rafting is a challenging recreational activity using an inflatable raft to navigate a typically fast-flowing creek or river.
bungee jumping: Bungee jumping (or "Bungy" jumping) is an activity in which people connected only by their ankles to a large elastic cord jump from a tall structure such as a bridge, tower or crane.
barefoot skiing: Barefoot skiing is water skiing behind a motorboat without the use of water skis, also referred to as "barefooting". Barefooting requires the skier to travel at higher speeds than is usual in conventional water skiing.
base jumping: Base jumping is an activity in which people jump from fixed objects, such as buildings or cliff faces, with a parachute that is unopened at the initial point of the jump.
kite landboarding: Kite landboarding is based on kitesurfing, in which a rider on a surf-style board is pulled over water by a kite. In contrast, kite landboarding involves the use of a landboard, which is a very big skateboard with pneumatic wheels and foot-straps.
jetboating: Jetboating is an activity in which people get a kick from riding a small boat propelled by a jet of water ejected from the back of the boat; the jetboat draws the water from under the boat into a pump inside the boat.
skydiving: Skydiving, also known as parachuting, is the sport of jumping from enough height, most typically from a small plane, mostly to deploy a parachute and land safely.

4. **Write a blog post about an adventurous experience you have had.**
Individual answers. The students will possibly be used to writing blogs. Those who are not can be helped by their classmates.

Films and Books

Neuseeland ist in Europa und der Welt bekannt geworden durch eine ganze Reihe von Filmen, deren Drehbuch bedeutende Romane zugrunde liegen. „Lord of the Rings", „Whale Rider", „The Piano" oder „Once Were Warriors" sind auch in Deutschland gut bekannt und werden im Internet vielfältig besprochen. Eine gründliche Filmkritik von „Once Were Warriors" legt zum Beispiel Alan Duff unter dieser Webseite vor: www.postcolonialweb.org/nz/duff/duffov.html.
Von den neuseeländischen Schriftstellern sind außer Kathrine Mansfield allerdings außer bei Fachleuten nicht allzu viele bekannt. Das Kapitel „Films and Books" ist geeignet, die Kursgruppe mit neuseeländischen Filmen und Autoren bekannt zu machen. Mit der Lektüre der hier vorgelegten Texte sollte nach Möglichkeit einhergehen, sich einen der vorgeschlagenen Filme im Original anzusehen bzw. eine Ganzschrift oder auch neuseeländische Kurzgeschichten im Original zu lesen.

I never knew this about New Zealand

Die Ausführungen in der gelben Infobox über den in Neuseeland gedrehten Kultfilm „The Lord of the Rings" und über weitere Filmproduktionen und Schauspieler soll die Schüler anregen zu weiteren Recherchen in dieser Richtung.
Dabei kann die Lehrkraft besonders gut auf die individuellen Interessen der Schüler eingehen und nach ihrem Vorschlag den einen oder anderen Film näher behandeln bzw. die Klasse Vorträge halten lassen über Schauspielerinnen und Schauspieler.
Der Filmstreifen am Bildrand gibt zusätzlich eine kurze Übersicht über die bedeutendsten Filme, die in Neuseeland gedreht wurden.

Films Important to New Zealand's Economy

Die Kinematografie leistet einen erheblichen Beitrag dazu, das kleine Land Down Under in der Welt bekannt zu machen, und stellt auch einen nicht zu unterschätzenden Beitrag zum Nationaleinkommen. Die in dem kurzen Text erwähnte Helen Clark (frühere Premierministerin, die die Bedeutung der Filmindustrie zu schätzen weiß) wird im folgenden Kapitel näher behandelt, sodass sich die Schüler hier voll und ganz auf das Thema „Film" konzentrieren können.

Whale Rider

Im Gegensatz zur einfachen Sprache des hier abgedruckten Scripts von „Whale Rider" stellt der Originalfilm recht hohe Ansprüche an die sprachliche Kompetenz der Schüler. Seines Themas wegen und weil er einen ausgezeichneten Einblick in die Kultur der Māori zu geben vermag, ist dieser Film jedoch sehr für die Behandlung im Englischunterricht der Oberstufe zu empfehlen. Gleiches gilt im Übrigen auch für den Film „Once Were Warriors".

Solutions

Activities p. 83

1. **What strength of character does Paikea reveal in this scene? Discuss.**
Paikea, the Māori heroine in this film, is a girl of about twelve years. Her grandfather has to choose a new Chief of their tribe. However, none of the boys has the qualities needed; only Paikea has. She has a strong will, she even dares to speak to all the people of her tribe, and firmly stands her ground with regard to the tribal traditions and is also very determined to lead her tribe into a good future.

2. **Work in pairs. Decide which NZ film or actor you are most interested in. Prepare a multimedia presentation about your choice. As a class, decide which film you want to watch. After viewing it, discuss it together.**
Individual answers. If there is no way to make a multimedia presentation, the class, together with the teacher, may decide how to present the chosen film or actor.
The discussion of the class about which film to see is one activity, watching it – another. The teacher must decide whether a final talk about the film is necessary.

3. **One of the world's greatest literary figures is Wellington-born short-story writer Katherine Mansfield. Make a poster about her life and work, about Witi Ihimaera and a third New Zealand author of your choice.**
The talks about New Zealand's most famous writers can be accompanied by reading one or two short stories. In keeping with this, the students should first find out more about the writers, talk about them in class and then read the texts.
Die Schriftstellerin Katherine Mansfield (1888–1923), die ihre Kindheit in Neuseeland verbrachte, in London studierte, später noch einmal für zwei Jahre in ihre Heimat zurückkehrte, um dann für immer in Europa zu leben, prägte zu Beginn des 20. Jahrhunderts eine neue Form des *essay writing* und wurde vor allem für ihre Kurzgeschichten berühmt. Ausführliche Informationen über Leben und Schaffen der Schriftstellerin enthalten zum Beispiel die mit vielen Links versehenen Webseiten www.katherinemansfield.com und www.ethnofilms.com/Katherine_Mansfield.html. Einen zehnminütigen Dokumentarfilm über Katherine Mansfield zeigt der YouTube-Clip www.youtube.com/watch?v=NtpKpKb7inM.

Zwei weitere empfehlenswerte neuseeländische Autoren sind in englischer Sprache auch im deutschen Buchhandel erhältlich:
- Roderick Finlayson: The Totara Tree (1838) – Der weiße, neuseeländische Erzähler R. Finlayson (1818–1892) wuchs in enger Gemeinschaft mit Māori auf und widmete sein erzählerisches Werk ihrer Kultur und Gesellschaft sowie den für die Māori-Gesellschaft destruktiven Einflüssen der *Pākeha*, also der weißen, europäischen Zivilisation, auf sein Land. In der Geschichte „The Totara Tree" lässt der Autor den Leser aus der Perspektive der Māori miterleben, wie sich eine alte Frau und mit ihr eine ganze Siedlung dagegen wehren, dass ihr *birth tree* gefällt wird.
- Witi Ihimaera: The Washerwoman's Children (1989) – W. Ihamaera (*1944) ist der erste Māori-Schriftsteller, der Kurzgeschichten und einen Roman („Tangi") veröffentlicht hat. In vielen seiner *short stories* reflektiert er Themen aus den Werken von Katherine Mansfield, so auch in der Geschichte „The Washerwoman's Children". Hier entwickelt er die Lebensläufe zweier Mädchen (aus Mansfields „The Doll's House") weiter, in denen sich die Kultur Neuseelands spiegelt: eine Frau bleibt in der Māori-Gesellschaft fest verwurzelt, die andere wird in England Richterin, bleibt aber letztlich ebenfalls den Māori-Traditionen verhaftet.

Die Seite http://de.wikipedia.org/wiki/Kategorie:Neuseeländische_Literatur enthält eine kurze Übersicht über einige weitere neuseeländische Autoren.

Politics and People

In diesem Kapitel lernen die Schüler einige wichtige Persönlichkeiten Neuseelands und die Arbeitsweise seiner Regierung kennen.

How Government Works

Vergleichbar mit anderen früheren Kolonien Großbritanniens weist auch Neuseelands politische Struktur einige Ähnlichkeiten mit dem ehemaligen Mutterland auf. Es ist auch möglich, einen Vergleich mit dem Nachbarland Australien anzustellen.

I never knew this about New Zealand

In der gelben Infobox werden auffällig viele bedeutende Politikerinnen erwähnt. Neuseeland war mehrfach Vorreiter in Sachen Gleichberechtigung der Frauen und ihrer politischen Mitbestimmung. Dieses Thema bietet sich erneut zum Vergleich mit Deutschland und der Rolle der Frauen in unserem Land an.

Central Government – Prime Ministers

Ein Interview mit der ehemaligen Premierministerin Helen Clark, die 2008 von John Key (*National Party*) abgelöst wurde, dient als Einführung in die Wirtschaft Neuseelands. In ihren Antworten macht Helen Clark deutlich, welch große Anstrengungen dieses Land *Down Under* im Bereich der Wirtschafts- und Sozialpolitik unternimmt. Nach der Lektüre dieses Textes soll den Schülern bewusst werden, wie gerechtfertigt es ist, im Untertitel dieser Oberstufenlektüre nicht nur in Bezug auf Australien, sondern auch hinsichtlich Neuseelands zu formulieren *„neither down nor under“*.
Eine ebenfalls sehr interessante Stellungnahme hat Helen Clark in der auch im Schülerbuch verwendeten Quelle (New Zealand Inspired. Southern Summer 2007) zur Bedeutung ihres Landes bezogen. Sie ist sehr gut geeignet als Stimulus für ein Unterrichtsgespräch oder auch als Grundlage für einen zu schreibenden Essay.

> “It is very easy for a small country on the other side of the world, to fall off the radar screen. I felt that we needed to avoid the ‘out of sight, out of mind’ syndrome.
> New Zealand is not a sleepy hollow, not a backwater. It’s a sexy and modern advanced nation. It’s a great place to do business with, it’s a great place to migrate to and live in, and on the international scene, it stands for something which is good and decent.
> We need to update the image so that New Zealand is not just beautiful, but also creative, innovative, safe, desirable. That’s it in a nutshell.” (H. Clark)

Women Play an Important Role

Um zu unterstreichen, was bereits in der vorangegangenen Infobox angedeutet wurde, werden hier zunächst einige interessante Aussagen darüber gemacht, wie Neuseeland seit 1893, als es als erster Staat in der Welt das Frauenwahlrecht einführte, die Frauen in alle Bereiche der Gesellschaft und auch in die Politik einbezieht.
Am Seitenrand werden die wichtigsten Parteien namentlich aufgeführt. Es ist sicherlich interessant, sie näher zu betrachten und z. B. die *Green Party* mit den politischen Grünen in Deutschland zu vergleichen. Voraussetzung dafür sind Internetrecherchen zu den politischen Kräften in Neuseeland, denkbar ist auch eine Zusammenarbeit mit dem Fach Sozialkunde.

Solutions

Activities p. 86

1. **How is the New Zealand Parliament elected?**
Parliament consists of the Sovereign and just one chamber – the House of Representatives. It is elected every three years. The current voting system, the Mixed Member Proportional Representation, was introduced in 1993. All New Zealanders aged 18 and over have the right to vote. Parliament has 120 members. In 2009, 37 of them were women and 16 Māori.

2. **Sum up what you have learned from this chapter about New Zealand's political system, and compare it to the British political system.**
The official Head of State is Queen Elizabeth II. She is represented in New Zealand by the Governor-General, as she is in Australia. The Prime Minister is the Head of Government, supported by a Cabinet of Ministers. The law-giving body is the Parliament.
Both New Zealand and Great Britain are parliamentary monarchies. The Head of State is the Queen. However, in Great Britain, there are two chambers – the House of Lords and the House of Commons. In both countries, the Prime Minister leads a Cabinet of Ministers which is responsible for everyday politics.

3. **Translate Helen Clark's answer in the interview (p. 85) into German.**
The students will, of course, translate the interview in different ways. The teacher has to decide whether the translation fits the original text or not. A possible translation can be found on the next page.

4. **How many women have a seat in New Zealand's parliament? Compare this to the number of female MPs in the German Bundestag. Do you think women play a big part in the politics of both countries? Discuss.**
In the information leaflet "New Zealand in Outline" it says that 37 out of 120 MPs are women. In the German Bundestag, in July 2009, 196 out of 611 members were women.

5. **Prepare a presentation on women in Aotearoa. Use the website www.stats.govt.nz. and the information given above.**
Individual answers.

Musterübersetzung
Helen Clarks Antwort auf die Frage „What are the top three items on your domestic agenda?"

Die wichtigsten drei Punkte werden die Stärkung der Wirtschaft, außerdem die Sozialpolitik und die Identifikation der Kiwis mit ihrem Land sein. Zum ersten Punkt, der Ökonomie: Ich glaube, dass jeder Mensch, der die Dinge objektiv sieht, sagen würde, dass Neuseelands Wirtschaft unglaublich gut abgeschnitten hat. Die Wirtschaft ist in ihrer Entwicklung weit vorangeschritten und imstande, mehr Waren und Dienstleistungen höheren Werts zu exportieren. Obwohl also der hohe Stand des Dollars nicht leicht war für die Exporteure, haben wir doch recht gut abgeschnitten, nicht zuletzt deshalb, weil wir die Wertkette nach oben geschraubt haben und in der Lage sind, die Preise eher zu machen als sie einfach hinzunehmen. Letzten Endes genügt sich aber eine starke Wirtschaft noch nicht selbst. Es gibt sie, damit man für die Menschen ein bestmögliches Leben garantieren kann. Wir agieren in der Sozialpolitik sehr proaktiv, was die älteren Mitbürger und Familien angeht, und auch sehr proaktiv bei der Schaffung von Arbeitsplätzen. Wir haben eine Arbeitslosenrate, die unter der von Großbritannien liegt, und wir haben eine ganze Menge getan für das Wohnungsprogramm. Eine Menge von Dingen haben sich verändert: vier Wochen Jahresurlaub, bezahlte Elternzeit und – und das hilft den arbeitenden Müttern und Vätern wahrscheinlich am meisten – wir sind weiter vorangekommen dabei, 20 Wochenstunden Freistellung für Kleinkinderziehung (pro Woche) zu bezahlen. Dann hat es da eine breite Debatte um die Identität Neuseelands gegeben: Wer sind wir? Wofür stehen wir? Wie zeigt sich das in unserer Außenpolitik? Wir erkennen das in den kreativen Künsten, in der Unterstützung, die wir unseren Sportlern geben, und in der Art, wie wir in unserem Land zur Wiedergutmachung des Vertrags von Waitangi stehen.

Not Just Sheep and Wool

Neuseeland ist vor allem stark im Export von landwirtschaftlichen Gütern. Jedoch hat es eine ganze Menge darüber hinaus zu bieten. Die beiden Seiten über die wirtschaftlichen Stärken des Landes geben einen Einblick, wie intensiv das Land bemüht ist, hochmoderne Technologien zu entwickeln und einzusetzen.
Vor allem die einfach zu überblickenden Statistiken auf Seite 88 sind durch die Schüler auszuformulieren und zu interpretieren. Die beiden auf moderne Technologien bezogenen Zeitungsartikel auf S. 87 sollten aufgrund einiger schwieriger technischer Passagen möglichst teilweise übersetzt werden bzw. auf ihr Verständnis bei den Schülern überprüft werden.

Innovative Economy

Das umfangreiche Feld der Wirtschaft kann nur an Beispielen abgehandelt werden. In zwei Artikeln aus der überregionalen Zeitung „The New Zealander" lernen die Schüler die fortschrittlichsten Projekte auf dem Gebiet „Windenergie" in Neuseeland kennen und erfahren in einem Artikel über das Elektroauto MIEV, das ab 2010 auch in Deutschland verkauft wird, dass die Regierung das Ziel hat, bis 2050 flächendeckend elektrisch betriebene Fahrzeuge einzuführen.
Darüber hinaus sollten die Schüler jedoch ihren Interessen entsprechend auch weitere Internetrecherchen über Neuseelands Wirtschaft durchführen.

New Zealand's Import and Export

Beim Lesen und bei der Interpretation der ersten Statistik („Sources of imports and export markets") kann der Part Deutschlands in der Wirtschaft von Neuseeland herausgearbeitet werden, aber vor allem die besondere Rolle, die Australien und die asiatischen Länder spielen.
Aus der *pie chart* der zweiten Statistik sollen die Schüler die Anteile der einzelnen Branchen an Neuseelands Export ablesen und sie verbalisieren.
Die beiden Abbildungen auf dieser Seite stammen vom *Agrodome* in Rotorua. Der *Agrodome* ist die bekannteste Schafschau in Neuseeland. Sie vermittelt einen ausgezeichneten Einblick in diese Branche der Landwirtschaft. Die Schau ist zu einem spektakulären Event für Jung und Alt, für Einheimische und Touristen geworden und findet das ganze Jahr über tagtäglich dreimal statt.

I never knew this about New Zealand

Die gelbe Infobox enthält weitere Angaben über Neuseelands Landwirtschaft und Industrie. Um nicht beim bloßen Lesen dieser Information zu verharren, können die Schüler diese und die vielen anderen Erkenntnisse, die sie den Lehrbuchtexten und ihren Internetrecherchen entnehmen, zum Beispiel in einem Poster zusammenfassen.

Solutions

Activities p. 88

1. **What are New Zealand's main sources of energy?**
   Australia's main sources of energy are hydro-power stations, geothermal power and wind energy. The country does not use nuclear powered generators. New Zealand's aim is to generate 90 % of its electricity from renewable sources by 2025.

2. **What does the import-export table tell you about New Zealand's trade relations?**
   New Zealand's strongest trade partner is Australia, followed by the USA. However, the Asian countries (Japan, China, and the Republic of Korea) taken together represent an even bigger proportion of exports to New Zealand than the USA.
   Germany exports about as many goods to New Zealand as China does, but nevertheless remains one of the minor trade partners of Aotearoa.

3. **Surf the web for more information on New Zealand's agriculture and industry, and then prepare a presentation on this topic.**
   The presentation can, for example, take the form of several talks given by a number of students or the form of a poster made by a group of students.

New Zealand's Nature – Beauty and Beast

Manche Menschen bezeichnen Neuseeland als ein natürliches Paradies (ein Ort heißt sogar Paradise), andere, wie George Bernhard Shaw im Angesicht der vulkanischen, heißen und beißenden Schwefelgeruch ausströmenden Quellen Rotoruas, vergleichen es mit der Hölle. Beides stimmt.
Die Schüler sollen diesem letzen Kapitel über Neuseeland entnehmen, dass es wunderschöne Landschaften und Erlebnisse bietet, andererseits aber auch Gefahren birgt: nicht durch die Fauna wie in Australien (giftige Tiere oder Krokodile kommen hier nicht vor), aber durch gefährliche geologische und klimatische Verhältnisse. Der erste Teil des Kapitels geht darauf ein. Der zweite soll mit der Schilderung von Landschaftsparks und natürlichen Sehenswürdigkeiten die Schüler anregen, sich weiter mit diesem Land zu befassen oder es eines Tages sogar zu besuchen.

New Zealand's Hazards

Nüchtern und ohne Übertreibung werden auf der ersten Seite dieses Kapitels die wesentlichen Gefahren aufgezählt: *drought, flood, snow, avalanches, storms, cyclones, fog, ice, landslides, tsunamis, earthquakes, volcanoes.* Die Schüler sollen sich über diese Gefahren informieren, ihre Bedeutung erkennen und eventuell mit der geologischen wie klimatologischen Geruhsamkeit in den gemäßigten Breiten Deutschlands vergleichen.

New Zealand's Beautiful Landscapes

Stellvertretend für eine Vielzahl von Naturparks und landschaftlichen Schönheiten werden fünf Gebiete in Bild und Text vorgestellt. Die Ausschnitte aus Zeitungen, Zeitschriften und Touristeninformationen sind jeweils so gehalten, dass sie einige wesentliche Informationen geben, aber auch zu weiteren Recherchen anregen.

Solutions

Activities p. 91

1. **Explain what the hazards mentioned on page 89 mean. Are they a danger to Germany or Europe, too? Discuss.**
   Not every one of the hazards mentioned above speaks for itself, for instance, snow. Therefore, the students are asked to define terms such as avalanche or tsunami. When comparing New Zealand's geological and climatic conditions with those of Europe or Germany, the students (or the teacher) might want to co-operate with one of the Geography teachers at their school.
2. **Sum up what the pictures and texts tell you about Aotearoa's landscapes.**
   New Zealand, or Aotearoa, boasts a variety of beautiful landscapes: vast plains and mountains, tropical rainforests and dry hilly areas, rural and urban districts, beaches and woods. It is this that makes the country so diverse and interesting.
3. **Make an imaginary trip to New Zealand and find these places on a large-scale map of the country: North Island, South Island, White Island, Rotorua, Taranaki, the Southern Alps, Mount Egmont, Mount Cook, Mount Ngauruhoe, Abel Tasman NP,**

Tongariro NP. Working in groups, search the web for more information about these and other sights, then make an illustrated map of New Zealand.
"Travel New Zealand ..." here means just to look at the map and find the places mentioned above, as these are some of the most interesting places to visit. The students could make an illustrated map of their own, in which they show these and other places of interest in New Zealand (cf. the map on page 66 of the Student's Book).

The Top Ten Eco-Experiences in New Zealand

Dieser letzte Text zum Thema „Neuseeland" bereitet die Schüler fiktiv auf eine Reise durch das Land vor. Der Text ist dem Magazin „New Zealand Inspired" entnommen und beschreibt in Kürze zehn wunderschöne, ökologisch gesunde Landschaften.
Die Schüler können sich vorstellen, sie bereiteten tatsächlich eine Reise in das Land Aotearoa vor. Um das letzte Unterrichtsgespräch zum Thema nicht mit Fakten und Daten zu belasten, sollte die Lehrkraft mit der Kursgruppe über ihre Vorstellungen von dem Land und seinen Leuten, über mögliche Reiseziele und -wünsche sowie über die Wahrscheinlichkeit, eines Tages – vielleicht als *backpacker*, über *work and travel* – nach Neuseeland zu reisen, sprechen.

Solutions

Activities p. 92

1. **These are the top ten eco-experiences which are recommended in a magazine. On your map, find where they are located.**
This easy task is a kind of good-bye to New Zealand, so to speak. It could easily be used as an introduction to a final talk about the country.

2. **Discuss and decide which of them you would like to visit. Give reasons why you have chosen this place in New Zealand.**
Individual answers are expected and can be included in the final discussion.

New Zealand Quiz

Ebenso wie im ersten Teils des Kurses „Australia and New Zealand" bildet ein Quiz auch den Abschluss des Themas „New Zealand" (s. **Worksheet 17**). Die Lehrkraft kopiert es entweder unverändert und lässt es die Schüler bearbeiten. Die Schüler können aber auch jeder bzw. jede für sich ein eigenes Quiz entwickeln und es einem Partner zum Raten übergeben. Die erste Variante berücksichtigt den behandelten Kurs insgesamt und ist wenig arbeitsaufwändig, die zweite lässt die Schüler aktiv werden und macht es möglich, den tatsächlich behandelten Stoff genauer zu berücksichtigen, ist aber zeit- und arbeitsintensiv. In beiden Fällen wird das spielerische Moment unterstrichen und die Motivation der Kursgruppe erhöht, wenn Preise für die meisten richtigen Antworten in Aussicht gestellt werden.

Worksheet 17

New Zealand Quiz

1. **New Zealand is comparable in size (270,000 km²)**
   a) to Greece.
   b) to Great Britain.
   c) to France.

2. **George Bernard Shaw is said to have remarked, "I was pleased to get so close to Hades and be able to return." Why did he say this?**
   a) The sentence is related to New Zealand's natural hazards such as floods, drought, and avalanches.
   b) In the days when Shaw visited New Zealand, the Māori were extremely aggressive and often killed white people.
   c) On the North Island, he saw frightening volcanoes and geysers.

3. **Aotearoa is Māori and means**
   a) "land surrounded by white water".
   b) "land of Māui".
   c) "land of the long white cloud".

4. **"Kiwi" is the nickname of**
   a) the NZ dollar.
   b) the New Zealanders.
   c) a bird.

5. **The Treaty of Waitangi was signed**
   a) in 1801.
   b) in 1840.
   c) in 1901.

6. **The Māori call non-white people in New Zealand**
   a) pouhaki.
   b) haka.
   c) pākeha.

7. **In schools, a prom night is**
   a) a dance party.
   b) a rock and pop concert.
   c) an event for alumni.

8. **The All Blacks is the name of**
   a) the indigenous Māori population.
   b) the national rugby team.
   c) the African minority in New Zealand.

9. **Bungee jumping began in New Zealand**
   a) in 1926.
   b) in 1956.
   c) in 1986.

Worksheet 17

10. Which of these is not located in New Zealand?
a) The Blue Mountains
b) The Misty Mountains
c) Mount Cook

11. Which of these films was not produced in New Zealand?
a) "Once Were Warriors"
b) "The Piano"
c) "The White Whale"

12. Keisha Castle-Hughes was nominated for an Oscar for her role in
a) "Avatar".
b) "Australia".
c) "Whale Rider".

13. New Zealand was the first country in the world to introduce the right to vote for women
a) in 1842.
b) in 1871.
c) in 1893.

14. Parliament in New Zealand consists of
a) the House of Lords and the House of Commons.
b) the Sovereign (i. e. the Queen or King of Great Britain) and the House of Representatives.
c) the Cabinet and the House of Representatives.

15. In 2002, how many more sheep than people did New Zealand have?
a) exactly five times as many
b) approximately ten times as many
c) almost twenty times as many

16. How much energy does New Zealand aim to produce from renewable sources by 2025?
a) about 50 per cent
b) about 75 per cent
c) about 90 per cent

17. New Zealand's principal export markets other than Australia are
a) the USA and Japan.
b) China and India.
c) Russia and the Republic of Korea.

18. New Zealand's highest mountain is
a) Aoraki.
b) Taranaki.
c) Tongariro.

Worksheet 17 Solution

New Zealand Quiz

1. **New Zealand is comparable in size (270,000 km²)**
   b) to Great Britain.

2. **George Bernard Shaw is said to have remarked, "I was pleased to get so close to Hades and be able to return." Why did he say this?**
   c) On the North Island, he saw frightening volcanoes and geysers.

3. **Aotearoa is Māori and means**
   c) "land of the long white cloud".

4. **"Kiwi" is the nickname of**
   a) the NZ dollar.
   b) the New Zealanders.

5. **The Treaty of Waitangi was signed**
   b) in 1840.

6. **The Māori call non-white people in New Zealand**
   c) pākeha.

7. **In schools, a prom night is**
   a) a dance party.

8. **The All Blacks is the name of**
   b) the national rugby team.

9. **Bungee jumping began in New Zealand**
   c) in 1986.

10. **Which of these is not located in New Zealand?**
    a) The Blue Mountains

11. **Which of these films was not produced in New Zealand?**
    c) "The White Whale"

12. **Keisha Castle-Hughes was nominated for an Oscar for her role in**
    c) "Whale Rider".

13. **New Zealand was the first country in the world to introduce the right to vote for women**
    c) in 1893.

14. **Parliament in New Zealand consists of**
    b) the Sovereign (i.e. the Queen or King of Great Britain) and the House of Representatives.

15. **In 2002, how many more sheep than people did New Zealand have?**
    b) approximately ten times as many

Worksheet 17 Solution

16. How much energy does New Zealand aim to produce from renewable sources by 2025?
c) about 90 per cent

17. New Zealand's principal export markets other than Australia are
a) the USA and Japan.

18. New Zealand's highest mountain is
a) Aoraki.